T0381438

Special Delivery

An interactive daily *devotional* revealing
God's powerful *life-saving* grace

ERYN YOUNG

WESTBOW
PRESS®
A DIVISION OF THOMAS NELSON
& ZONDERVAN

WestBow Press books may be ordered through booksellers or by contacting:

WestBow Press
A Division of Thomas Nelson & Zondervan
1663 Liberty Drive
Bloomington, IN 47403
www.westbowpress.com
844-714-3454

Scripture taken from the New King James Version. Copyright © 1979, 1980, 1982 by Thomas Nelson, Inc. Used by permission. All rights reserved.

ISBN: 979-8-3850-2090-4 (sc)
ISBN: 979-8-3850-2091-1 (e)

Library of Congress Control Number: 2024904705

Print information available on the last page.

WestBow Press rev. date: 06/05/2024

Dedicated to all who have encountered uncertainty in the midst of struggle, yet kept walking while awaiting delivery.

The ability to read this makes two things true. God brought you through it and that makes you Special to Him

Edited by JeNean Lendor

* "Always give a testimony of what the Lord has done for you, as that is often your best ministry"

Preface

While this is not my first book, I hope it's a valuable part of my life's work. Don't get me wrong, though I am an extrovert that actively seeks new adventures to conquer, I tend to spend more time than I'd like to share analyzing/reflecting on life.

As you will soon see, I have had a very innnnteeeresssting life.

In my 30+/- years, so far I've had at least 8 dramatic near-death experiences (that I know about) yet I'm still here! I have also been blessed to be used to save two people's lives. While it would be heroic to say I used muscle or wisdom to do it, the facts are that a "cat" and confiscating a bottle of bleach helped me save them. Weird right?

For example, those around me sometimes tend to accuse me of being accident-prone, given my substantial brace/ bandage/ crutch count. I, however, disagree considering the ratio of dangers and situations the Lord saved me from compared to the periodic "consolation" nicks & scratches that occur. I'm learning to see that crutches are not so bad when considered a tool of grace.

A few disclaimers for events that you will read, I've already talked to God about them and therefore, take them as accounts not justifications. His grace is definitely amazing but also not governed by presumption. What you should know is that there are three ideas that are fundamental to my upbringing:

1) Do not be limited by the word "can't"

2) Being open to adventure is a valuable avenue of learning - not to be replaced by only reading books.

3) Prayer changes things, so defer to that when tempted to over-estimate your abilities (*What a blessing to have a mom who is a prayer warrior*).

Living a life marked with randomized irony co-mingled with divine blessing, whether I deserved or understood them or not just seems to be what has kept me sane and is my story. For example, despite surviving my 1st Whitewater rafting expedition with only three of a six person minimum, add in a few car accidents one that was headed for sudden death having rolled three times on a busy freeway, being so scared a rabid dog would kill me as a kid that I leaped completely over a 7 ft long car (a 1970-something Nova), interestingly, the 1st time I ever broke a bone was when I fractured my toe by bumping it into the curb while running into the house. Before you point fingers grace works both ways, thankfully. Like the largest scholarship I received in school was one I never applied for... I'll let you be the judge (Just don't forget about the whole "judge" not lest ye be "judged" thing....)

Special Delivery is a sometimes funny, hopeful, thought-provoking, usually ironic journey of a devotional with real-life experiences and key points from sermons that have got me through.

I've even included the testimony of a few loved ones from my "how I got over" village, who have overcome trying circumstances as well.

My hope is that I can help you see that the kind of God who loves me through ALL kinds of stuff will also guide you through whatever mixed bag you are carrying. What I'm coming to learn 30-something years later is that the journey to Him is just as important as the destination, and through it all He has a spot with your name on it!

*Opening quote by Pastor Bobby Mitchell

Contents

By Topic

You may have noticed no specific story numbers, relax it's intentional I realize that we all experience life differently. So while this is how I organized it, what better time to bring back the *Choose your Adventure* story format as a message followed by one from another section may be of more benefit to you. In the spaces to **LEFT** of the title write in the order you choose. After finishing a Section, in the space to the **RIGHT** the way you would re-order it. I'd love to hear feedback about the changes to the given section and why. Connect on Socials **#specialdeliverydevo & IG @Eyoungspeaks2**

Spirituality w/o God has way to many I's

Others

On Christian Life an Consequences

On Purpose

Cloud of Witness

Poetic Recuperation

A Little Extra

Section I

SPIRITUALITY W/O GOD HAS WAY TO MANY I'S

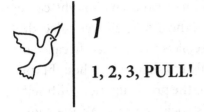

1

1, 2, 3, PULL!

And do not be conformed to this world, but
be transformed by the renewing of your
mind, that you may prove what is that good
and acceptable and perfect will of God.
Roman 12:2 NKJV

What comes to mind when you hear the audible sound of counting? Go on, I'll give you a few moments... Though I'm sure your answers will vary, I don't think I'm alone in saying that typically the mind lulls a little as you're progressing toward at least the five or ten preparing for the next ... something you know will happen. Around... still afforded a small gift of delay before having to perform, right?

The case was not so in a film that debuted in 2002. Now right off the top, you may not be familiar with the phrase "1, 2, 3 PULL!" unless you recognize it from the famous movie "My Big Fat Greek Wedding" which much to the surprise of many people's expectations took the box office by storm. Whether it has come to mind or not, you should know that the phrase was well used throughout the movie by the main character's aunts. Not as a rallying call to complete some insurmountable task, but to actually serve as motivation for them to simultaneously draw in and muster the energy to "pull or lift" up whichever effects of weight, age, life, or diet left on their body and to simply smile for nearly every picture taken of them at the wedding. While those scenes usually brought about a good laugh for those watching the film, a random thought came to mind, despite having not seen the movie in over a decade. While the memory of the clip replays in my head because of its popularity, I'm oddly compelled to share a few thoughts on the topic as it ironically relates to the preoccupation with self-observation/elevation in today's social culture. While those were mere fictional characters, I can't help but notice the similarities that exist these days in "reality". You know, the way that people manipulate backgrounds and often risk their life to capture and repost in daring places (really, lady... a selfie in front of a lion cage). If that wasn't dangerous enough, you would be alarmed to know the increase in pedestrian vs. car accidents due to texting while walking because someone just had to "update" their post.

What is really with the immediate need to convey perpetual greatness? Simply put, to as in the movie "1,2,3 pull" their ordinary circumstance to provide pristine images of "everything's great pix's" for others to stare at, like and hopefully have enough meaning to derive a favorable comment. I'm not saying that the cure is in releasing the good and bad in an open display to the public, or that it's not okay to find a way to wear a smile when you are going through though times. However true reality generally doesn't read like an all-year paid vacation. Life will undoubtedly bring circumstances to take you as far out of the comfort zone as possible. But when we include that added layer of overconsumption of self or you find yourself bathing in the fluff created by others doing the same we can easily be detracted from actually experiencing a life of abundance. A better option is to actually be open to the will and moving of God around you so that we can receive the level of fulfillment that others have only Posed and posted about.

Going back to the movie, the flip side of this habit, if not corrected, is each time those Greek aunts discovered that once gravity happens what was so fervently pulled, inevitably falls and it is the same with social media culture. After the post button has been clicked, consider how you feel once things have settled and the mask falls off. You are back to, loneliness, un-fulfillment, and grief.... If you are not at peace and your rest is disturbed, it's probably time for you to unplug and push away from a lot of worldly time-consuming preoccupations and reconnect. Whether it's through individual prayer or surrounding yourself in the fellowship of positive family or spirit lead believers such as a weekly Bible study or other small groups and take a chance on the opportunity to encounter safety and serenity in the perfect will of the Lord.

As You Go...

While creating posts online for social media is a popular way to pass the time, what are a few other hobbies that you enjoy that connect you with people in real life?

_____

_____

_____

_____

Describe at least one benefit you would have if you periodically substituted scrolling for socializing?

E.Y. Reflection
#1

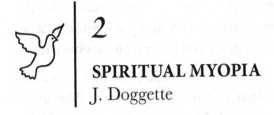

2

SPIRITUAL MYOPIA
J. Doggette

**And when thou pray/give/fast, thou shalt
not be as the hypocrites are: for they love
to pray standing in the synagogues and in
the corners of the streets, that they may be
seen of men. Verily I say unto you, they have
their reward, go into your room, and when
you have shut your door ... and thy Father
which sees in secret shall reward thee openly**
Matthew 6:5-6

Key Points

<u>Myopia</u>- The ability to see the things in front of you but not from afar.

<u>Hyperopia</u> (The antonym) – The ability to see things afar off but not up close.

My Reflection

I heard this sermon my first year in college and it remains etched in my mind. It still feels like a fresh word in spite of the thousands I've heard within the last 15yrs. It was impactful as it occurred right on time at the beginning of the year. A term used by one of my favorite speakers Dr. James Doggette, that I had never heard before. Ok, you ready? The term was spiritual myopia. While you would earn a lot of "impress your friend" points, it gets better with the explanation.

When you think about it, how many times do we find ourselves so focused on the things in front of us that we can become oblivious to our surrounding and get caught off guard by things going on in the background? The number would be alarming. No, not, ever vigilant you, right? Ok, perhaps you'll reconsider when you prioritize your to-do list vs nurturing relationships. Things like texting while/walking /driving/watching your kids or even your individual quest for holiness vs positively impacting someone around you…?

I can't speak for everyone but it reminds me of a situation I encountered. I had a favorite hat that I loved to wear because it gave me a chic yet artsy cool look. I'm sure if you randomly located pictures of me for a good 2year span in my early 20's you would find that hat in half of them. One day I had to go pick up some tickets from a shop located in the Wilshire district in LA. I was having issues finding parking on the busy street and didn't have a lot of time to spare so I parked on the opposite side of a street with at least six lanes. Initially, I made it across okay, yet my attempt to get back to the car was like a scene from a level of *Frogger* (google it millennials).

As I was dodging cars, it came to a point that it was clear that I had to run to make it back to where I parked. As soon as I began to run, my favorite hat leaped off my head and fell onto the street behind me. When I felt the air on my scalp I did as my many years of athletic training conditioned me to do which was to react instantly. So I turned to mad dash thinking about how much I love that hat and, hey I'm quick enough. However, before I could get my other foot into the street a truck sped by and ran over my hat. I jumped back to the curb, though I could hear the crunching of said favorite hat I, was instantly overcome with gratefulness (and honestly fear) for my life being spared. I wouldn't be honest if I told you that I got in the car and went directly home for a stress cry or nap. I probably should have, but the truth is that I sat and waited for the street to clear and retrieved it. Though a few cars were thoughtful enough to swerve around it, I opted to keep the hat to this day, unwearable with its tire stains and all. I keep it as a reminder of how silly it would have been to have been to be run over for the sake of just a hat.

(J. Doggette Sr., Sermon notes,
Madison Mission, 2000)

As You Go...

Consider your current situation and if there are things that are clouding your view and what types "ruined hat" reminders can you set in place?

_____

_____

_____

_____

Instead of missing the spiritual/relational/ individual forest for the trees, let's determine to refocus our vision by remembering to;

1. Slowdown 2. Step back to gain a different perspective 3. Be a thinker instead of a reactor. 4. Take time for Bible study and prayer as it gives the capacity to see in front and behind us with an eternal perspective.

3

TO HYPOCRITE OR NOT TO HYPOCRITE, THAT IS THE QUESTION?

**And when you pray, you shall not
be like the hypocrites....
Matthew 6:5-18 NKJV**

When I was a kid I must admit that I was not a fan of reading. Yes, obviously the ability to read was necessary for everything especially when it came to school. I'm pretty sure this is the reason I was not a fan of adding it to my list of hobbies which included T.V. However there were some items that never fail to motivate my interest in or curiosity for inhaling words. My fascination for Archie comics, writings on candy wrappers, and that interesting facts could usually be on the back of my church school lesson and Bumpers stickers, kept my mind going.

I'm sure I've dated myself with the first one (Hey I earned the years so) and just in case you judge me for the 2nd one let me point out that *Laffy Taffy* and *Bazooka Joes* had great content. By the way, if you recognize any one of those names then chances are I found a friend in classic candy, and you know you liked them too. When I read today's verse it instantly brought to mind a quote I came across. The sticker said "It's better to walk alone, than with a crowd going in the wrong direction" by Herman Siu.: It's not flattering but it does speak to how the appearance of something positive does not inherently make it so. Sure standing up in the most visible spots to make eloquent professions alleging to communicate with God seems great. However, when it comes to talking to God, the fact that He is omniscient, meaning that before we can even bring our mouths to move, He heard about it around the time you recognized a need.

Our circumstance may not always reflect the answer to our prayer in the time, direction or extent that we recognize but that does not mean that God has not already formulated an answer. There is a lot of wisdom in the second half of that text especially when you respect prayer as two way communication vs. a request line. Sometimes the answers we are searching for can be claimed in the words and feelings of assurance. Which God is so willing to provide to those who will linger a bit longer.

The thing that is to be feared in the situation with the hypocrite is similar to the problem with the crowd described in the bumper sticker scenario. It is that, by drawing more attention to yourself then to the God you profess that you talk to. Beware as you're more likely to get swept up turning sincerity into performance.

As You Go...

Consider a few reminders offered from the Bible:

- God is sensitive to our needs and he slows down or picks up when we need it.

- Prayer must be appropriate when it's used correctly

- We've been trained to be good religiously. However, being a Christian is of far greater Importance. Following the actions of Christ not only does well for self-improvement but perhaps the greatest benefit of prayer is towards the building up of those in the communities around us.

- Matt 20:28-34 Shares that, "Just as the Son of man came not to be ministered unto, but to minister, and to give his life for many".... The verse also includes the healing of the two blind men, whose faith healed them after they heard Jesus passed. They recognized him as not only someone special but that He was the son of God and would not keep quiet until they got His attention.

What are a few things that are weighing on your heart that you need to take before God in prayer closet time?

_____

_____

_____

_____

If we were given only 30 min of time to talk directly to God per day, how would it change the way/content/seriousness you used to talk to him? When would be the best time to schedule that meeting?

_____

_____

_____

_____

E.Y. Reflection
#2

4

THE GOLDEN SHIELDS ARE GONE!
M. Woodson

Now it came to pass, when Rehoboam
had established the kingdom, and had
strengthened himself, that he forsook the law
of the LORD, and all Israel along with him...
and it happened in the fifth year ... Shishak
king of Egypt came up against Jerusalem
because they had transgressed against the
Lord... Then Shemaiah the prophet came
to Rehoboam... So the leaders of Israel and
king humbled themselves...the word of
the Lord came to Shemaiah saying "They
humbled themselves, therefore I will not
destroy but grant deliverance... So Shishak
king of Egypt came up against Jerusalem and
took away the treasures of the house of the
kings: he took everything. He also carried
away the shields of gold which Solomon had
made. Then King Rehoboam made bronze
shield in their place, and committed them to
the hands of the captains of the guard, who
guarded the doorway of the king's house.
2 Chronicles 12:1-10 NKJV

Key points

1. Golden Shields-Are character, courage, faith, fidelity found in the walls of our souls.

2. Environmental Christianity- Is when you start to think that because you were raised around Christian surroundings you have your golden shields by osmosis.

3. The way we live our life will either erode or strengthen the integrity of our shields.

4. In verse 10, Gold was replaced by brass. Gold in the Bible (is faultless, pure Righteousness.) Sacred special to God, golden candlesticks, golden mercy seat, Ark of the Covenant (golden mercy seat),

Don't substitute bronze for gold

Gold	Bronze
Obedience	Objectivity
Love	Legalism
Sacrifice	Your Fruits (like Cain)
Faith in God	Being Faint in heart

5. Don't become settled and satisfied or make no effort to replace the areas in your past that are brass but started out as gold.

6. Revelations 3:17-18 Reveals how God is a God of balance. Because you say "I am rich... and have need of nothing – and do not know that you are wretched, poor, blind and naked. Verse 18 encourages us to know that God is always available to" buy from Me gold refined in

the fire, that you may be rich... that the shame of your nakedness may not be revealed"....

When trials come they are here to purify the gold that God already placed in our souls.

(M. Woodson, Sermon, Fifty Fourth St. Church, 2005)

My Reflection

This message reminds me of a not so bright moment from my childhood. I'm a 80's baby so there is an entire thankful decade of my peers who are so grateful that technology wasn't advanced enough to record everything. I grew up in the house with two older brothers in the middle of L.A. on a one-parent income which also paid for us all to receive a Christian education for the majority of our lives (Thanks Mom!).

With that being said, as you can imagine, by the time I got in middle school funds could be tight from time to time. At some point I was alerted by the pains in my toes that it was time for some more shoes. To give you a little background I was one of a handful of girls at my school that took recess and P.E more seriously than most other subjects. After weekends of sharpening my skills at little league practice and watching the Showtime Lakers, I figured it would be wrong to allow other kids to get away with attempts to beat me in "play time" sports. Sorry Joel it's always go time, Ryan Let's go!

It became more than apparent that I needed some new shoes. I was getting excited about all the possibilities of which pair of Nike, Reebok, and I would've even settled for British Knights to grace the school with. So I tell mom that I'm looking forward

13

to a trip to the mall. Well nope, there was none of that. In the meantime I had to settle for wearing my other causal non tennis pair and instead spent the time socializing with the non-active friends on the other side of the playground.

My hopes were brightened the day we went to pick up the shoes. We made our way to the store and though I wondered why we passed several *Foot Lockers* without stopping, my expectations were dashed when we ended up parking in front of the Payless store.

Now I know what you're probably thinking but it's not that they Weren't a good company it's just that, well, let me continue. After dragging up and down the aisle without finding one that fit mom's price point and my interest, my mood changed. Let's just say I was given some sobering options which had me circle back to one which most closely resembled Nike's. Well, partially Happy. With a few efforts to try to blend in discreetly at school, I went back to playing sports and things were great. No one seemed to notice my non-Nike's for maybe about a week.

Unfortunately, around week two, after an intense basketball game, I started noticing my feet were getting hot so I found a way to slide away after finishing the game. I quickly took off the shoes so my feet could cool down. The discomfort was enough to try and return those shoes, to from whence they came, however it didn't stop there. The next day I returned to my favorite game but this time I figured taking it down a few notches will help me avoid the same issue.

To add insult to injury, after being called in from recess, I overheard friends laughing and talking about something funny they saw on the court. While I had not seen what it was, it was enough to peak my curiosity because, after all, who doesn't like a good laugh? So as the next break came, I went straight to the court walking because, I'd learned my lesson about running in those shoes. I was mortified to find random streaks up and around the ground!

That theme from that *Southwest Airlines* commercial about wanting to "get away"

couldn't even compare to how I felt. :/ The only saving grace that did not give me away was that these shoes happened to have the standard black sole which meant the guilty party could've belonged to any number of kids out there. Let's just say the next few weeks were spent either being injured or not feeling well and away from the court until things died down.

While I couldn't have called that outcome as a kid, trying to hold out as long as I could in ho I could, in hopes of getting what I valued in my little world (even though misguided) was important enough to risk either continued pain. Or the result of not following the very clear option whispered in my ear while at the store. The opposite is true with God and His ability to provide us the best delivering us from ourselves. However, we often find ourselves in life's maze bumping into roadblocks because we are running ahead looking for low-hanging fruit or cheaper ways to get through. But the Bible says in the book of Hebrews, run the race with endurance... looking to Jesus...the author and finisher. (Hebrews 12:1-20)

As You Go...

Perhaps that's not your thing and you fall in the group with Christian's content to blend in with the crowd or go to the places everyone does/drink the same drinks/live with people who don't belong to you. After all, it's now a "who are you to judge their actions" type of world... But the God we serve can see every possible outcome at the same time. While the consequence of every bad decision may not be evident to you or immediate. The continual habit unchecked can lead to the erosion of your sensitivities to make sound judgment calls, which like a frog in a gradually warming pot will lead to your demise.

What brass have you exchanged for gold unintentionally?

_____

_____

_____

_____

The good news is that God is a forgiving God, so how can you make efforts today to get back what the locust stole? (Joel 2:25)

_____

_____

_____

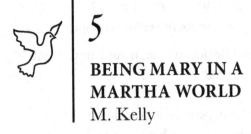

5

BEING MARY IN A MARTHA WORLD
M. Kelly

**She had a sister called Mary, who sat at
the Lord's feet listening to what he said
Luke 10:39 NKJV**

Key Points

1) Busyness is demonic, it's sinful to be as busy as we are. Jesus had more to do than anybody but He never expressed it as busy or in a hurry to do things.

2) In the Woman at the well story, Jesus was on the way but He didn't rush in the process. The Woman with the issue of blood came and though he looked too busy, she had the faith to know that just touching him would bring change. She got it and Jesus even stayed and fellowshipped with her. 2 Peter 3:9 says that the Lord is not slack concerning His promises... but is long suffering towards us.... With Mary and Martha, there is the right thing but you should never lose sight of the fact there is also a God thing.

3) While we are busying about prepping for the Lord to come we don't want to miss out on having authentic experiences with Jesus (at his feet).

4) One of the devil's great tools is not that we lose our faith but that we settle for mediocre versions of spirituality.

5) Having a full schedule doesn't mean your important, it means your imbalanced.

> Focus on teaching people to slow down
> and appreciate Jesus who is here and build
> your relationship with Him now and not
> running in the kitchen (like Martha).

(M, Kelly, Sermon notes
Mount Rubidoux, 2009)

My Reflection

A lot can be said about the catch 22 of busyness. But the message that was preached was a complete explanation on it so I'll move in different direction. What struck a nerve for me was the fourth point on how the devil uses settling. In plain ink, it has a way of appearing clear cut and perhaps even so much so that falling for it would be too obvious. In real time, however, I'm afraid it is an entirely different thing. On a daily basis, there are usually several things vying for our attention. The truth of your intentions, however positive or negative is that distraction is a limitation of being finite.

It was at some point after college that I found myself in a good place. Having a nice balance between working, spending time with quality friends, volunteering, and even managed to still have free time. When I had free time I watching the Lakers or playing my favorite, basketball. How could you go wrong with exercise hidden behind a game which is also entertaining? One of my favorite places to play at the time was a local gym run by my friend. It was fun, close and connected to a church so also safe. Safety is definitely a plus. Outside of that I was good at it and not to mention that little detail made for a great ratio for single an adult keeping her eyes open ;).

One particular night while having a good game I heard a voice on the sideline that initially came off as a heckler well hater calling out as I passed by. Well it actually turned out to be some guy actually giving compliments. In-t-e-r-e-s-t-i-n-g! This has never happened before but ok, thank you stranger. The next game began and pretty soon compliments turned into helpful tips every time I came down the court. Right as I was about to give this annoying person a piece of my mind for an unsolicited attempt at validation, I looked up and... hello.

Yes our eyes met and I was pleasantly distracted by his brown eyes, bright smile, caramel skin and the chiseled features that came with him. What followed after was a request for my number, earlier gym meetups, frequent conversations, mutual compliments and a new found appreciation for this cute, talented, funny, charming also respectful guy. Well as time passed by and after checking his background through a mutual friend, I began to feel comfortable with spending time with him in person. I offered a few invites to church events, but he seemed to always have reasons that he couldn't make it, except for the time when he joined me at a church league basketball game.

Initially, I didn't think much of it. After all I was not ready for church member interviews, as if he was coming to pop the question before even saying hello.

The next time we attempted a date, we planned to meet at the park after work, with no real plans but to soak in the day and each other. However that didn't happen and after a-what-is-this, fallout, things normalized and we began talking about attempt number two. I was due to perform at church so I again invited him. Yes the guy who came looking for me, somehow only had a lame excuse to offer in return. It's foggy now but it was along the lines of "that I'm Catholic and am not really supposed to go to other churches." ...very suspect. After I refused to let it go as I had many catholic friends who could never. It eventually came out that he's "not into church, like that."

That was the yellow flag for me and though we slowed down, my distracted self continued continued to communicate with Him as I reasoned that it was the Lords job to bring him into the church fold. There were mutual feelings but since we never kissed, it never got serious. Later that night I got a call I'd never forget. The short version was that after talking to our mutual friend as he put it "I understand that you are a good girl and I know that I am not that kind of guy." I'll spare some of the details "I don't want to be a guy that messes you up with my intentions." Whaaat? Who says that?

Now, I'd love to say that, that was the red flag, hallelujah, and I'm-out of here! ... Moment because that answered the "is he the right guy for me" question since it was "message from the Lord" clear but ...no. Yet again I didn't' let it end there. While I am not proud of the moment, I turned it into a do you really think you have that power over me competition. By the time the talk was over we, well I pushed us towards settling for friendship instead taking the free and clean let him "ride off into the sunset" pass. We gave it a break for a week and decided a nice game of basketball, which is where it all started would be a nice way to kick off this new friendship thing. However, while playing attempts at just playing the game was still more than expected.

Outside of the valuable lesson that physical activity plus attraction does not equal friendship, I praise God for His forgiving grace despite our ignorance. Looking back, not only did he win the "we wrestle not" battle, I (the regularly churched one) somehow still ended up leaving the defeated one in the situation.

Perhaps that's why the concept of being Mary in a Martha world hit me differently. Despite all the churching, Jesus, and wrong vs rights I had in this situation, he became the standard bearer that the Lord spoke through to call me out. It's one thing to choose humility and an entirely different thing to be humbled. I guess there's something to the whole verse about taking heed unless you fall! It became abundantly clear how easily people fall into what most consider "perfectly normal" relationship behavior which I'm sure awaited every "casual" date that we planned but couldn't' seem to make (probably grace).

I'm grateful to say that this scenario brought life to what the Take 6 song that says "something within me that holdeth the reigns and I can't explain." This has kept me ever since from assuming laurels or even morals would protect me where the will of God didn't' bring me.

As You Go...

1) What could be that "rock crying out" situation have to be in order to get your attention?

_____

_____

_____

_____

2) How could you pray for support in reconnecting with Jesus to loosen the chains that surround you?

_____

_____

_____

_____

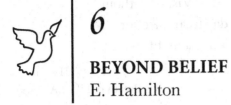

6

BEYOND BELIEF
E. Hamilton

Send men to spy out the land of Canaan,
Which I am giving to the Children of Israel;
from each tribe of their fathers you shall
send a man, everyone a leader among them."
Numbers 13:2, 27-33 NKJV

Key Points

1) If you believe in God for great things, why wouldn't we ask for them? Sadly, we try to pacify God by thinking lowly of Him. One example is Caleb and Joshua's report of Canaan. Numbers 13:33

2) God will sometimes show you an opponent to show you how much mightier He is.

3) Your outcome is sometimes developed by your thoughts. Bible shares "For as he thinks in his heart, so is he. As he thinks in his heart, so is he." Proverb 23:7

4) Walk by faith. There are people in your life waiting to see the evidence of what you profess.

5) Vision is the bridge between your past and your future. If you are going to make it to the next year. You have to activate your faith.

Chinese Proverb – Vision without
action is a daydream. Action
without vision is a nightmare.

(E. Hamilton,
Breath of Life, LA, 2019)

My Reflection

History nor politics have never been subjects that have ever been on my favorite list. However, since searching quotes and sayings for hidden meaning is, every now and again the two meet, and the value of a few of those shifty characters gets redeemed. For example, I may not be able to recall Sgt. Colin Powell's contributions outside of his title, but I can share how one of his quotes has had a positive impact on my life. O…K you ready for it? No, it's really good… (cue the introductory horns) "Perpetual optimism is a force multiplier".

I can't see whether or not you shouted about that. I could understand if I said it but when you consider that it came from a decorated army general you have to admit it brings a lot more color to the party!

While I may not recall the context the fact of the matter is that I have found bursts of motivation throughout the years by simple recitations. In those times when used as a declaration, it has meant that if I can keep my attitude and actions focused on the bright side despite what the evidence, situation, and people with reports say. likely to more likely to galvanize traction from the momentum and others going the same way.

I remember when (thought cloud & story chair please?) there was an annual church competition that a group of us 20 somethings and a few youth at my church wanted to enter. As one of the older churches in our region, we made sure we had a team nearly every year, this year however we received registration details late which put us in bind. We had a few feasibility meetings with the pastor and youth leader to determine if we could prepare only a month. Given those factors and the small detail that a team hadn't yet been selected, they decided that it was not a good idea, and they couldn't support it. After the shock and disappointment wore off a group of us who were still interested got together and considered how we would go forward after all someone had to represent that church. So we prayed about it and what started as a few courageous "We can do all things..." people slowly rounded out to enough for a team and a few willing to take the lead.

A study guide was given with assigned parts and a strict schedule was given for reading and quizzing and encouraging each other by our appointed group leader. Initially, we met under the radar for given times to block outside distractions since it was clear that we were on our own. What was consistent was that every time we met we prayed that the Lord would be with us & help us to commit only what was needed to memory. Finally, the day arrived for the event and we canceled our plans to study twice, I believe that a few even fasted and we joined fifteen other churches in the competition. The game started without a hitch well minus the fact that some of the naysayers decided to show up despite... I digress. As the rounds progressed we found ourselves either being the first with the answer or among the top three with the correct answer. Before long we looked up and there we were in the finals with only a few questions to go. Ironically we noticed that other teams that didn't advance seemed to have A study guide to work from, an option we were not afforded.

I won't delay the results much longer as the point exists beyond it... in the end, we WON! The game involved being prepared for any line of questioning from one entire book of the Bible. What's interesting however is that outside of the gladness of being able to bring the trophy back home (having not won in like 10 years) was the look on the faces of those who doubted that entering in the first place was even worth it? Our small team was surprised and more importantly, God got the glory. He was faithful in both granting us the victory and sending a reminder to those in leadership as one of the favorite verses which in some "special" way found its way into my assigned section. "I say keep away from these men and let them alone, for if this plan or this is a work of men, it will come to nothing. But if it's of God, you cannot overthrow- lest you even be found to fight against God". Acts 5:38, 39

That was additional proof that the Lord was truly working through us to bring the vision that we could not see, into reality. Without finger-pointing or rehashing, we felt it would be best to be gracious and allow ALL from our church to be a part of the congratulatory picture.

As You Go...

As Christians we are all called to a relationship with Jesus, what are 2 things that you feel is keeping you away from being in partnership with him on some things in your life?

_____

_____

_____

_____

I don't want to call the situation we dealt with turning enemies into your foot-stool since they were church members. There is something to be said about dealing with doubters. Describe an act of faith in the face of doubt that required endurance that has made an impact in your life?

_____

_____

_____

_____

You never know how sharing will impact lives
of another, until you try. Revelation 12:11

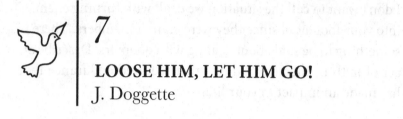

7
LOOSE HIM, LET HIM GO!
J. Doggette

And many believed in Him there.
John 10:42 NKJV

Key Points

1) "And I know that you always hear me, but because of the people who are standing by I said *this*, that they may believe that You sent Me." John 11:42

2) "And he who had died came out bound hand and foot with grave clothes, and his face was wrapped with a cloth. Jesus said to them, Loose him, and let him go"…. John 11:44

3) We are to be Jehovah's witnesses as Christians, called to point people to God. Don't get caught up in titles, as the function that you serve is just a means to an end.

4) When the question "where have you laid Him? Was asked John 11:34. What He was saying was, at what point did you give up on Him?

How to Bring Restoration

1) When it comes to evangelism, it does not start with the people we don't know, but with us and the people we put in "imaginary graves."

2) Say a prayer then make a list of people you put in the "grave" and pray for them before you go and mess up their lives.

3) Take away the stone; Jesus made them take the stone, because you put it there. "You have to undo what you have done." In some cases, you have been the stone.

4) Think about a person who no longer attends church. If you find anything that you could have done differently; ask God to give you another opportunity to "lose someone" and allow them to receive the same grace He has allowed you.

My Reflection

Perhaps above all of the admonitions the term "imaginary graves" stands out. Wow, while it may sound a bit oxymoronic, to put it into context, consider popular cute lies like "sticks and stones can break bones, but words will never... Yes hurt. Another thing that is far too often perpetrated is that church is a place for "perfect people". Though the last one may not be verbally stated. How often have you heard people say that they, just are not ready to come to church yet. As if our efforts at cleaning up or fixing our problems were a requirement. As if whatever desire was holding back their return to church exceeds the peace found by reception by a loving God. As He is the one actually able to heal that longing?

I wonder if you took an inventory of what caused people in your past to step away from "following God or leaving the church." Whether you grew up with them and are no longer around. Or you may see them around other places but notice a disinterest in talking about Jesus or Christian-related things. We could probably trace their departure to the same list of "invisible" non-tangible issues across the globe. I'll start with some that I have had first- and second-hand knowledge with multiple decades of regular and active involvement in the church:

- Unkind rebukes for wearing clothes that don't fit the "Holy" appearance.

- Patronizing or poor treatment of people at first judgment,

- Church folks who would rather side with all things traditional, neglecting the person in the process.

- Quick and judgmental words to a young or new Christian instead of loving-based teaching and encouragement, allowing God to make the correction.

The descriptions can go on, but I believe the picture is becoming clearer, and it hurts my heart that at least one person's life is altered by each example. Despite the level of visibility of the harm, if we do not acknowledge the damage done by words and change the actions, we express towards the children Jesus died for. Then we are basically tying them to chains that would weight them down to a very literal grave. The scripture says in Romans 3:23 that "ALL have sinned and FALLEN SHORT of the glory of God."

The good news, however, bears far more importance for those who have felt cast aside or don't feel that they fit in the "church or with Christians." Or just as in John 44. Make room and let Jesus come into our situations that are dead or showing no real evidence of life, He will command sometimes the very ones who allowed bondage holding you back to be loosed and let go. Even now, we can name what or who has an "invisible" hold on you and endeavor to daily claim His promise that" I have come that we may have life, and they may have it more abundantly. John 10:10

Sermon By:
(J. Doggette, Sermon note
Madison Mission Church, 2001)

As You Go...

Which bound person can I
call/ text to encourage?

_____

_____

_____

_____

8

BE FRUITFUL!
D. Snell

...Then they brought to Him one who was deaf and had an impediment in his speech, and they begged Him to put His hand on him...And they were astonished beyond measure, saying, "He has done all things well. He makes both the deaf to hear and the mute to speak"
Mark 7:31-37 NKJV

Key Points

1) God has asked us to stop being comfortable being just functional when He has called us to be fruitful.

2) An example given was the Bible's story of the healing of the mute, pointing out the action connected to the attentiveness of the believers present. While the believers were present and around Jesus, an understanding of the mute persons situation and his inability to receive due to his condition moved them to take him straight to the feet of Jesus.

3) Though the story does not specify, it's clear that the combination of their faith in what Jesus could do with God's ability led to his healing. We then must ask ourselves the question of whether or not this miracle

would have had the opportunity to occur if the friends were content to just attend the same congregation of people listening to Christ that day?

4) When we pray to God to speak to us, it's not that He speaks louder; sometimes the actual answer to the prayer is the removal of the things that keep us from hearing the word of God clearly.

(D. Snell, Sermon notes,
First Church, AL, 2022)

My Reflection

If I were to ask you, what are two of the most important attributes in the life of a true Christian? I could almost guarantee the majority will quote James 2:20-22, which speaks on how faith without works is dead! And while you are not wrong, as it's clearly in the Word, I did a little research as we wouldn't want to let the efforts toward a Master's degree fall out of practice (beats back nightmares of APA reference proofing). However, I discovered some interesting facts, that you may find surprising to know. The words PRAY, HEAR, FAITH and Work appears at 547, 516 (824 w. listen), 257, and 400, respectively.

Despite the shock in my baptized curiosity, I would guess that it is because faith can be built through praying; and once you've heard from God, you will be better equipped to accomplish the work He has for you. And the evidence of all four in concert should establish your relationship with Christ's outward "membership" as an authentic Christian. While I don't claim to know all the answers (like the accusation from a popular viral video interview), like the music artist, my conviction is based on my experience actually hearing from God.

I realize that phrase may make someone feel some-kind-of way. Though I don't offer any apologies, as it was frequently mentioned in the Bible. I will share that it's not all the time (as I know I'm a work in progress, prayers appreciated) I am glad God continues to speak. When I've listened, I've encountered many saves by His grace!

I realize you can't pick up the bi-product of belief without receipts, so O.K. Okay, I'll share a few (and collect my poetic snaps later☺). Though the delivery methods differed, I assure you they were unmerited. I am sooo! Grateful! I landed on the right side, and this time I'll keep it brief. Email me if you're curious and need the rest.

The accident-aversion store: In short, three friends got into a car excited about plans for what would have been a short trip. A few things got moved around in the car to make us feel more comfortable, and a basic prayer got thrown up, and off we go down the hill except... Wait, why aren't we stopping? And as the barricade continued to approach, all eyes closed, the wheel turned, and somehow only the side of the car was grazed. We walked away uninjured; and we never again underestimate how dangerous something sliding under the brake could be. Praise God for the wonderful power of His grace to answer even a haphazard prayer.

The Big Box Character Depot

I accepted the call to act as background for a popular TV show called "Yo Mamma". On the show people receive prize money for insulting people. It was interesting. I was young so I happily agreed to go and look alive as the camera roles, in the background. However, when I made it to the set. I was approached by a producer who offered me an opportunity to make more money that day. I reluctantly asked what I would have to do? He then offered to upgrade me to be a contestant instead of an extra like the 50 other people there. I could use the extra money at the time. While I usually deal in smiles and sunshine one of my secret talents is having an immediate comeback. I can be armed and ready to one up a person with insults or dip words into so much sarcasm that what I meant would be realized a few hours later. Amid my pause to respond, I heard a still small voice tell me to say no, reminding me that while I was in a secular space I needed to act like the Christian I professed to be... And with that Divine whisper, I thanked the guy and he went on to the next person.

Two months later the show aired and I stopped checking for the program as I rarely saw myself on TV. Around the same time a group of youth from my church were scheduled to travel to a national youth Christian conference in Atlanta to represent our churches and bring back a report. Thankfully we arrived safely. However before we could get out of the airport I was stopped by one friend and two random people who kept looking my way. One eventually came over and began to ask if I was the girl on the TV show? After verifying the name I said yes, and I was shocked at how I was found among the other 50 people. Then a few laughs and questions about how I got into the show followed and the day kept moving. Before that weekend was over I was stopped about 10 more times and I am Sooo grateful that I said no to making more money. Had I accepted the producers offer, to throw venomous insults, that same amount of people would have seen the negative influence as not only an intro to my character but also a poor representation on my home church that I was representing. Praise God for the way of escape!

When I got home from the conference, I caught that episode and it is still the show that I have had the most appearances in. The fact that it's also been in syndication and has several thousand view on YouTube still amazes me. Talk about divine irony, or in this case intervention. But also a testament to upholding character when you think no one's watching. I'm glad that I can respond with Thank You Lord instead of turning my head in shame every time the episode crosses the screen.

As You Go...

Have you ever encountered experiences where you heard from God? If so how did it manifest (voice, impression or etc?)

_____

_____

_____

_____

Regardless of the experience you listed, how do you think that encounter did/or could have impacted the way you live out your Christian walk

Section II

OTHERS

I'm sure by this point in your life you have heard the saying curiosity killed the cat. Well… in my experience responding to curiosity has saved two strangers and a squirrel actually. Talk about Special Deliveries of the three situations literally involved cats now that I think of it. #Thestoryofmylife. No really I couldn't make this stuff up. Let me testify to you how in his infinite wisdom somehow His sense of humor picks broken vessels as prime users.

9

OTHERS PT.1

For the Son of Man has come to
save that which was lost.
Matt 18:11 NKJV

Fill in the blank, Jesus loves _____. If I were to ask everyone in a room full of 100 people to stand up if they answered "me" you'd at best probably only have two people sitting. Seriously you can almost pick any place in the Christian world and you could almost guarantee the same result. Why is that though? I mean don't get me wrong, it's a profound truth that is fundamental to being a Christian, some would say. To know that an all-powerful God, who's creative power is so dynamic as to split a sea clean down the middle, while at the same time simultaneously being gentle so as to protect us to "not let our foot dash, against a stone" when an army comes against us, against His will. Psalms 91:12

Yeah, it sounds pretty safe to say that our parents did us a favor by letting that song or text be the first thing committed to memory about God.

I do wonder well I'll put it this way. Currently, all you have to do is turn on anything with a live feed and within 5 minutes you sadly will be bombarded with "breaking news." News of human lives injured and far too often lives are lost due to gross abuse of power. Whether it be short-sighted convictions of entitlement, or children being forced to learn evasive techniques in conjunction with the common core. Or awaiting the next rage-filled gunman walking up and blindly spraying the classroom. There is also, unfortunately, the many pages that can be filled with the incessant negative comments displaying any segment of the population that disagrees with many who can easily be characterized as narcissistic governing leaders of what I'm told is the "free world." It sometimes makes me contemplate how or to what extent our treatment of others throughout history would be different, if the word others were swapped with me as that same fundamental truth of, who Jesus loves.

No, it doesn't have the same cutesy ring to it, but consider the potential value of having an early understanding that God loves those around us. Whether they look or feel, smell or act like us. Yes it's true! And for no other reason than others like me were buried in His heart from before you were a thought in your parents eye. Declaring that "before you were born I sanctified you...." (Jeramiah 1:5) Universally it may not be the most popular opinion or practice, but He Does! No really He does? He even pushed past the spiteful fear of the unknown and different than usual treatment of himself. He sacrificed His life just to give the rights to access The Kingdom for "others." The Bible is full of examples of the extent that men and women of God pushed past their conveniences and traditions to stand in the gap or make bold moves extending opportunities to experience life and liberty.

As You Go...

If there ever was an example to practice patterning our lives after, wouldn't Jesus make a good model? I wonder what changes would happen in our world if we tried putting others first even just half of the time starting today, What do you think would change?

_____

_____

_____

_____

E.Y. Reflection
#3

10

OTHERS #2
Squirrrreellll!!

He shall call upon Me, and I will answer him; I will be with him in trouble;

I will deliver him and honor him.
Psalms 91:15 NKJV

It was the best of times, it was the worst of times just kidding. Well it was actually a good day. It happened to be one of the days of the week where I was able to work from home, which always is a blessing to me and my gas tank. Any who, I was in the house doing something between paperwork, watching a show and typing when I heard a strange sound. Initially I dismissed it as one of my phones or other devices probably dying. However the sound persisted and even seemed to get louder. I decided to get up and investigate and ended up going into my front room. At this point I picked up the closest heavy thing I could potentially protect myself with. I mean I don't know how -scary a squeaking thing could be but it's not supposed to be in my house, it's gonna have to get out one way or another. Now back to the story.

After careful discovery, I found that the noise was actually outside… Thankfully. With the heavy item still in hand, I peeked out through the window and found a large cat intently staring at something. It was moving around and then returning to the same spot. It was disturbing as, we don't own a cat and he looked very comfortable. Secondly, what in the world is he looking for as it is probably ours because its our yard. I guess that's still point one, and two. Cats do a lot of things but squeaking is not one of them, so now my curiosity is on fire and I have to go out. So with my back up item I open the door and now said cat is watching me watching him. The stare down continues and so does the squeaking that is distracting the both of us.

I closed the doors so that whatever the 3rd party is, does not cause us to pack up and move. After finding a safe distance away from the situation I look over to find that the sound is coming from behind a small cabinet that we keep on the patio. I start eyeballing the cat who has now found a new position closer to the cabinet, I bend over and Squirrrreeeeeellllll!!

Whaaaaaaat! There's sooooo many questions, like who knew that the sound they can make is a squeak and oh my goodness this poooor little guy is out here literally screaming for his life as the cat has got him cornered. Literally, if it had not been for an inch sized gap where he was hiding; the cats arm would easily been able to reach this lil guy, whose new name would have easily been lunch. I snap into action as I'm pretty sure I could take a cat. So I let out a shout and began running after him which thankfully worked as I would have hated to use my item.

Over the fence and out of the way goes the cat and I went back to go find my new little friend. Still scared even though he stopped squeaking and I'm sure I saw the little guy shaking. I don't know if it's because I watched to many Dr. Doo Little movies but I told him or her "ok, you're good to go, which did little to inspire him. That didn't work since apparently, squirrels don't speak good English. I opted to move the cabinet and it slowly came out and ran across the yard. As I watched it go, ensuring that the cat was not watching. The thought of wait, what in the world just happened passed and I started laughing and shaking my head (SMH) at the thought that this is the type of stuff that only happens to me. The bigger picture dawned on me that I will probably never forget, which is … If A God that is (as Stevie the Wonder says) millions of light years away found this squirrels situation important enough to trouble the mind of this human, who "just happened" to be home, who just happens to have a life-long sense of curiosity to be a part of the squirrel save, Then how much more is He able to deliver us from the things that seem too hard to bear.

Yes life is sometimes scary and unexpected, bad things can happen, you don't always know what's around the corner. But when God promised to cover you with his feathers (Psalms 91:4) or storage cabinet to keep you from harm, believe that He will. Never be ashamed to pray or even squeak until God has dispatched a choice vessel to aid and assist in a rescue mission just for you

All I could do the rest of the day was to continue to SMH but also praise Him for the privilege. It's amazing how something that was little for me, meant everything to that little guy.

As You Go...

Identify a few things that you could do to make a little space to do daily, weekly or monthly that could be impactful to something/someone else and try it who knows the reward could be heavenly!

Daily

_____

_____

_____

_____

Weekly

_____

_____

_____

_____

Monthly

_____

_____

_____

_____

E.Y. Reflection
#4

11

CAT CRYING IN THE WILDERNESS

My sheep hear My voice, and I
know them, and they follow Me
John 10:27 NKJV

A few years ago, we went on a family trip to the mountains to relax for a bit and soak up some fresh air. As most people know, California is not really known for obvious seasons or extreme weather, so it was a nice change of pace to get a few days of snow in December. Outside of your typical vacation, there was great food, lots of pictures, and fun things to do. By the time the day was over, we were so tired and content to relax and soak up some TV.

After getting comfortable, I heard a noise outside that I initially thought was a cat the piqued my curiosity and also irritated me to keep it 100...honestly. I heard crying in the forest that just wouldn't stop making noise. I continued to listen, wait, turn volumes on things down, and cross-checked with others in the room. Still puzzled, I decided to look out the window, and wait, is that a lady? She was also vacationing in the Snow ridden Lake Arrowhead Mountains.

After we alerted security and helped them locate and rescue her, she shared what happened. Apparently, she took a shower after her husband left, she put a robe on, and went back to the balcony to smoke. At some point, she closed the glass door to keep the smoke out of the lodge. However, after finishing she pulled the sliding glass door to return inside and found the door somehow managed to lock her out. After trying several things unsuccessfully, she defaulted to screaming for help. Four hours later, in 30° weather, we found the lady barely standing, pale shaking, and leaning up against the balcony rail; hoping to spot anyone passing. Her consistent cries for help had died down over time to what we could at best interpret as a cat whining. We were so happy to watch the security team wrap her in a blanket and stayed with her until her husband returned. The next morning, when she met us, she was in tears, profusely thanking us for taking the time and interest. She told us that she had prayed but was literally on the verge of giving up.

Ironically, while she was asking what she could give us to repay the kindness, I'll never forget the overwhelming feeling of gratitude and shock that the Lord would see fit to entrust us with "just happening, to be in the right place," tasked with being a part of His promise to deliver us. Even 8 years later, just recalling the thought is still humbling and brings to mind how we often take for granted the gift of not only having faith in God but that sometimes He also extends chances to demonstrate faith in us.

As You Go...

Looking back over experiences in your life, are there times that you have encountered that caused you to reach outside of your comfort zone as a result of following Gods lead?

_____

_____

_____

_____

If so, did you run into something unexpected? Did you learn something new about yourself or God as a result?

_____

_____

_____

_____

When you find yourself in circumstances that seems to not go as you plan. Try stopping to consider that maybe what you think is an annoyance, is actually an override. An opportunity from God to assist or restore life for another one of Gods creations.

#pause #pray #listen but also #move

E.Y. Reflection
#5

12

PAIN RELIEVER + BLEACH = A LIFESAVER

Be (SALT)- Join the Save Another Life Team

You are the salt of the earth: but if the salt loses its flavor,

How shall it be seasoned? It is then good for nothing

but to be thrown out and trampled underfoot by men

Matthew 5:13 NKJV

Ever had a day where you wake up, and whether you feel well or not, would rather do anything but roll out of bed and go to work? Despite the struggle that day I made my way, and the majority of the day went well. However, somewhere around the midday, my body started to rebel. After checking my pockets for pain medications and coming up dry, I made a B-line to the car and then back to the classroom. I walked in to check the bag I brought in that day. Well, after going through every single pocket as if my life depended on it (I felt like it did), there was no pill; only a saved vitamin, which is not helpful in that situation. Things were getting bad, and it was time for reinforcements, so legally owed. My supervisor cleared my break, and I rushed to the nearest store to grab and bring back the reliever that I needed.

I arrived at the store, grabbed my item off the shelf, and made it to the checkout line; quickly, as there were not many people in the aisles. Just as I was getting excited about the odds of actually making it back to work in the 15-20 minutes I requested, I noticed something odd. The people in front of me, would randomly leave the line to go to the window of the store. They would watch, shake their heads, and come back and say something to the person they came with, and then they would alternate and do the same. This piqued my curiosity, despite not hearing music or witnessing any reactions that called for my fight or flight sense to kick in. By now, I'm sure you have begun to realize that it doesn't take much for my curiosity to take over. Anyway, where was I? Oh yes, so I paid for the Aspirin and also joined the crowd at the window. After taking in the scene outside, it didn't take much time to join the others in shock and disgust.

After the initial shock and confusion subsided, I inquired if anyone had called the police, to which they replied yes. I was puzzled to find that no one even stopped what they were doing or looked bothered to do anything more. The group just continued to record the videos of the activity on their cameras, pointing, staring in awe, and reacting. What happened next, I can't say came more from being mad at the unconcerned click-baiters; or from being a first responder for so long. But I decided to approach the lady.

I didn't really have a plan, but knew something had to be done as there was something very wrong with the 30ish lady; picking up a 64-ounce jug of bleach-filled commercial cleaning fluid and drinking it as if it were juice! I was horrified to watch her drink until she physically couldn't, followed by her stopping only to vomit violently, drink more, and again turn and vomit!

I sent up an ok, help me, Jesus... Then went over and asked, "What is going on?" She kept the drinking going, ignoring me the first few times, but eventually, when I'm guessing I annoyed her by not going away; she stopped long enough to rest after retching as it seemed there was nothing left in her stomach. Now upset, she clearly did not appreciate me distracting her, so she shouted, "I hate my life, and I don't want to be here anymore!" While those words still shock me to this day, I was a bit confused. Though I couldn't understand, for her to choose this painful way meant that whatever led her here had to somehow be worse than what she was doing.

It also occurred to me that, the fact that she did this publicly left enough of a gap for hope or will to live. So, when I asked her to stop, sharing that she didn't need to do this, she interrupted, shouting, I do! Though it felt a little tug-a-warish, I replied No... You don't!, things can eventually get better. She went directly back to the cleaner and took a swig, so it seems that she didn't believe me and, like clockwork, started retching. Well! I tried reasoning with her, but that didn't work. And I can't say I had this planned, but as soon as she put down the jug and turned, I grabbed it and ran to the car.

Yes, I stole her bleach and drove off... Let's call it risk management, to save her life. As I drove off, I could hear her shouting choice words; however, I continued to make my way to the nearest police office, where I left a report and directed them to the location where the incident occurred. After all the commotion, I returned to work a bit in shock, trying to process everything that just happened. I made a B line to my bag, cracked open the bottle, and finally got a chance to take the medications I purchased.

Before returning to my workstation, I unzipped a pocket inside my bag to store my pill bottle and was amazed to find pain-relieving medications sitting in clear sight. Yes, the exact bag that I searched feverishly from top to bottom only about 30 minutes before; the very action that sent me to the store in the first place.

To this day, it baffles my mind. I even asked coworkers to look in the pocket to verify that I wasn't seeing things; they also confirmed. God is always in need of vessels and though we continue to ask Him to perfect our character or wait to be given a great responsibility. But we often miss the opportunity as it can be disguised detours in life. A quote a friend recently used in her sermon comes to mind, she shared that. "We are the change we've been waiting on, we don't have to keep waiting on anybody else"-Kimberly. Mann

As You Go...

There are so many things to take away from that day, so I'll leave it between you and the Lord, but I will share that I was meant to be at the store at that time. The other thing I can confirm, and it's as sure then as it is now, is that God works in mysterious ways, His wonders to perform! Roman 11:33. In Psalm 37:23, the Bible says that the steps of a good man are ordered by the Lord. Though the status of where we may fall on the "good scale" may waver, one thing that stays the same is that God is always interested in the use of vessels for His will.

A question we must pray and ask ourselves: Are you available? Or will there be a busy signal?

_____

_____

_____

_____

E.Y. Reflection#6
#theAsprinmiracle

Section III

ON CHRISTIAN LIFE
AN CONSEQUENCES

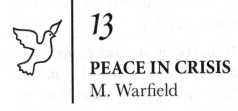

13

PEACE IN CRISIS
M. Warfield

On the same day, when the evening had
come, He said to them, "Let us cross

over to the other side."
Mark 4:35 NKJV

Key Points

(On Jesus speaking to the waves while on the boat with the
disciples)

1. The storms were happening with Jesus on the boat with
    the disciples.

2. When sitting on the shore you won't experience any risk
    but you also won't witness many real triumphs.

3. Sometimes we may be aware that He is there, but forget
    that He is Sovereign and all-powerful. Safety consists
    not in the absence of danger, but in the presence of God.
    What we need to do is ask God to remove the fear, not
    the furnace. Like Daniel, or like Paul to remain in the
    jail cell, as He is still working.

4. The position Jesus took in the boat should have been
    enough to give them the same calmness in the storm.
    We get in the way because when we're working, He is

resting. It's when we're burned out or stop that He can do His best. Take your hand off His business!

5. Think about it, if He could show so much power in the storm (even over nature) in response to their fear, how much more could He do when He responds to them in faith?

6. We're going to face many trials but we can have peace when we keep our eyes on His face. 2 Corinthians 4:8, 9 shares that we are "Afflicted but not crushed, cast down but not destroyed."

7. Know that He can turn a virus into a victory. Remember He who goes with you! Mark 4:36... Your life is on display. Their response with Jesus was a witness to the other boats and ours must be the same if we claim He is with us.

Be reminded that the name of your Savior is Emmanuel (God with us), and you can have peace because He is the Prince of peace!

(M. Warfield, Sermon
Grand Ave, 2020)

My Reflection

This message touches me deeply every time I come back to review it. On its own, the words the Lord gave his servant for this one at ANYTIME I believe were appropriate. But given the fact that it was received in the middle of the uncertainty, and for some fearful, Coronavirus outbreak in early April 2020, I have to say it came down like fresh squeezed juice at the end of a long hot day. So many things stand out. For now, I'll focus on the statement that as Christians we should remove the fear-stricken way that we sometimes navigate life. "If in the storm He (God) could show so much power (even to change nature) in response to our fear, how much do you think He can do if we responded to Him in faith. We can have peace because the God that is with us is the Prince of Peace."

I don't know if you have ever been in a situation where someone's had to come to your rescue. If you haven't, don't feel bad. Despite being the youngest sister with five brothers and one sister, the first time I needed saving was while drowning. Ironically, none of my siblings were there to help. Help came from a friend who was younger and smaller than me. Thanks Tim! But that's a story for another day! #brothers4sale #Buytradeorbarter. While I don't recommend learning to swim on the 6-foot side of the pool as an option for things to put on a to-do list, God blocked it and Thank you Lord!! For the sake of the message let's go with a less traumatic situation. This situation occurred while playing basketball in high school. During a weekend team tournament where we encountered an interesting event where another type of saving was necessary.

After traveling several hours by bus our female and male teams were ushered to separate wings to set up for the weekend. As usual, the girls finished first and after taking a walk around campus, a friend of mine caught the eye of a guy from one of the opposing teams and asked if he could call her at the dorm where we stayed later. We all smiled and were happy for the prospects. However it wasn't long before word got around to everyone else.

After a few immediate callbacks on the lobby pay phone (yes it was late 90's) which went unanswered, due to my friend's "big brother" blocking her from getting the phone. The phone was eventually answered by a random guy on the team who was not involved who got a rude message and a declaration from the interested caller (now upset) male, our teammate laughed and hung up the phone. The upset male called back and shared that he (the teammate answering the phone) would see how funny it will be when they came over to our building! While sitting with the rest of our teammates I'll admit that we were both shocked and a bit confused about what to expect. However the guys, assured our chaperones that they would only go outside to talk and not fight.

Things were all fun and games sight unseen. Looking back I'm sure "mister tough caller" and his two or three friends might have felt confident in their position because we were in their comfort zone. However, they came towards where we were staying, and found the said "big brother" and entire boys' team were standing on the steps patiently waiting. Only a cartoon could accurately display how wide their eyes opened.

I'll never forget how quick the march turned into a stride, and their bold declaration into a stutter which sounded more like a question. To paint the picture clearer, they could have been the big men on their suburban, year-around boarding school campus. But, though none of our guys truly intended to fight, at least three of the eleven boys from my school were above six feet, grew up around Compton (Google it if that means nothing to you), and never missed a meal.

Thankfully, given the... I'll go with "surprise", the misunderstanding was cleared up and everyone agreed to focus on the game instead of exploring "who" originally answered the phone.

As funny and unnecessary as that whole situation was, isn't it true that we too convince ourselves that we can handle issues that arise when we perceive them to be manageable? We can even get to the point that we spread that same surety to others.

Be it overcoming a bad habit, accomplishing a goal or, trying to create peace in a disturbing situation. However, because we don't take into account that there is a real enemy at war for our peace and our soul we will almost always find ourselves under-matched and in compromising positions.

We must always remind ourselves that we serve a God who is bigger, ever-loving, and Sovereign. And while you may get hit with some clouds and even rain as we travel through this sin-sick world if we have truly allowed His presence on our boat He that is with us is truly the only one able to keep us from sinking...well as Jude 1:24 puts it falling.

As You Go...

Our days are often filled with constant concerns that will distract us from operating from a resolve that God will deliver and take care of us.

So what things, system, or maybe even which types of people could we surround ourselves with to help us re-focus in times of uncertainty?

_____

_____

_____

_____

14

WHAT PEOPLE WHO FOLLOW CHRIST KNOW

...You may understand my knowledge in the
mystery of Christ which in other times was
not made known unto the sons of men...
that the Gentiles should be fellow heirs,
and of the same body and partakers of His
promise in Christ through the gospel...and
to make all men see what is the fellowship
of the mystery which from the beginning
of the ages has been hidden in God....
Ephesians 3:4-9 NKJV

Key Points

1) The Christian who knows who they are does not have to worry about what they are not.

2) They can answer quickly and with certainty.

3) They can remain calm and unmoved by their surroundings.

(Sermon notes,
Madison Mission Church, 2001)

My Reflection

On this occasion, the preacher emphasized that affiliation is often connected with association and how our lives can be affected as a result. I am almost 100% sure that you have at one point or another had your parent or guardian question or caution who you are going to be with when you were making plans "with friends" as you were leaving the door. Or, in those situations where you have invited someone over to visit but others in your party are not familiar with them.

The line of questioning usually begins with cues on first and last names, then travels to where they are from and how you met them. And yes, while it comes off as an interrogation session, the goal is usually well-intentioned with goals to look out and protect you or to form a reference (for safety).

It's almost an undisputed fact that people usually feel more comfortable releasing others to "strangers" when there's some type of known connection (e.g. that's James the mailman's son etc.).

While reference offer some point of comfort, I've also had experiences that can balance that scale a bit past solemnly relying on comfort. While growing up I enjoyed a lot of the cool things that happened during the summer in Southern California. Like time on the beach, going to theme parks after paying your dues a few hours at a summer job and waking up when you felt like it being freed from school. Some Summers I and one of my siblings would go travel to visit my dad for a few weeks. Without fail in addition to what felt like visiting everyone he knew at some point we would get the come "go with me to work" call that happen soon after sleep began to get good. He worked as a carpenter for many decades and while you could never be sure when it would drop... It would and regardless of what your thoughts for the day were ... cancel them. You were going to get real hands on pain... I mean experience from hours of learning how to drive a hammer at any angle, set drywall or anything else that was being handed to you while he was building.

Though there was clearly a difference of perspective in what the vacation in the title Summer Vacation meant, after many years of the same I learned to appreciate the ease at throwing projects together without having to ask for help even now. Well, except for the time in my twenties while casually talking to a friend of the family who was hosting my internship (thanks Lanus!). She was sharing some renovation plans while walking through the house, so I thought I'd share a few tips to make the changes more cost-effective. I shared that I watched and even helped my dad and other family do it for years. Things changed entirely when she said that it would be a great idea then asked for the times that I could come on over and help the team that would soon be coming to start the job.

No that was definitely not the intention of the reference, I did however call her attention back to who the actual professional was. To reiterate and yes clarify my actual level of comfort I shared that I'm sure he wouldn't mind offering her troubleshooting, giving her his contact info then offering that I could be available as an EXTRA hand if needed after that point. My level of comfort regardless of position, in relationship may have offered some value in soft credit but even in that example, it is only as beneficial as my ability to provide a link to one who can actually provide the help that another stands in need of!

Conversely, how should being called children of God impact the way that we approach life? Outside of the common "would you go the same places" spiel that people like to go to, would we add more eternal facing task to our things to-do list as now we are being cognizant that were wearing our Fathers jersey/ uniform?

When the difficult times hit harder or more frequent then we like, after a healthy amount of time emoting, could we work on a default action of actually taking the concern to prayer and leaving it at His feet be the new default action we do? The Bible is filled with quotes on Jesus' references to us as daughters and of God's. Since, we often so quick to proudly proclaim that we our Christians meaning followers, let be intentional about handling our problems the way that Christ did. Mark 1:35 shares a great example of His prayer habit. In the morning, having risen a long while before daylight, He went out departing to a solitary place and there He prayed.

As You Go...

In the case of this message, how much of an impact would truly be made by accepting that our Father is the Ruler of heaven and earth? Would we go about the actions of our day in the same way, or would we steer away from certain things? Or should we?

_____

_____

_____

_____

Even more importantly, would failure or inadequacy throw us as far off track if we valued God as Sovereign and under the control of everything around us?

_____

_____

_____

15

ROAD KILL AND A PRAYER

"It shall come to pass, that before they call, I will answer; and while they are still speaking I will hear"
Isaiah 65:24 NKJV

♪ Now this is a story all about how my car got flipped and landed with the right side down. It'll take a few minutes so hang in there and I'll tell you how my life was spared by God from road kill by a prayer! ♪

Look, I may not be a famous rap artist from the 90's, but I think that's not too bad for an intro. Sooo, what started out as a road trip to spend quality time with family that we don't often see, turned into an unforgettable experience that not only changed my outlook on life but solidified the miracle working power of God. All of this within a matter of minutes!

After a great visit, my brother and I were making our way back from Northern California. While driving on the freeway, I noticed an odd sized animal on the road that I didn't want to hit. As I tried to move back to the lane, the car began to fishtail (sway) forcing us to figure out how to fix this alarming situation. I made one more attempt to steady the wheel, and instantly the car started flipping. Yes! On the freeway. I can't say my life flashed in front of my eyes, but I did send up some urgent prayers. I sent up prayers for my brother, who had upcoming major plans that I didn't want him to miss, as well as for myself.

I wish I could tell you that what happened next was a blur but unfortunately I recall every flip.

Now let me turn it around and shout, as in retrospect, the ability to remain fully conscious after surviving an accident where the car flipped over three times is more than a blessed miracle.

Bonus Miracles

1) In His grace, He caused sovereignty to impact the physical, allowing for part of the freeway that could've been an overpass that we would have gone over to be a ravine that stopped us from continuing to turn.

2) Though there were plenty of cars on the road with us, we hit none of them.

3) When the car landed on its side, we were only about 300ft away from the freeway entrance, which can be open season for unsuspecting drivers, yet none of them hit us.

4) The car didn't catch on fire.

5) Neither one of us suffered any broken bones, despite the car being totaled.

6) That happened to be one of the few times we used the extra funds to pay for the rental car insurance, so the car was covered.

7) And possibly my favorite is Isaiah 65:24 affirms the priceless value of a praying mother. Now, just in case you were thinking I already covered the prayer part of the title, Ohhh you ain't seen nothing yet!

The nurse asked if there was anybody we needed to call. Okay, so let me set the scene. We were being hauled off in the ambulance while we were away from home at about 2 a.m. Talk about stress. Even though we were over 21, the answer was clear: call mom! I wrestled the number out of my pocket while on the gurney and got nervous thinking about how worried she would be. I was concerned about the dangers of shocking her with the bad news at that hour. Imagine my surprise when she answered and responded to the news with a calm voice. She assured me that we would be fine.

"Whaaat?!?! Um, are you okay?" She prayed with us, and the other family members who came here to be with us including my brother Justin who surprisingly got to the scene before the ambulance. My mom then said to call before they discharged us and got off the phone. Though still in pain, you can now add confusion to the list. They released us, I called mom back and rattled the update to her then asked how she managed to be so calm despite the situation

Her reply still brings chills. She shared that she went to bed early that night and randomly just woke up. She didn't know why, so she looked around and didn't notice anything, so she got out of bed and prayed. After getting back in bed, she said she felt at peace, so she laid back down. Within about 10 minutes, she received the call from our older brother that we had been in an accident and were okay but we were at the hospital getting treated. OHHH, YOU CAN'T TELL ME, WE SERVE A GOD WHO'S NOT GOOD, BUT ALSO THOROUGH!

As You Go...

Do you have any before you call for testimonies? If so, what happened, and how did God bring you out or through?

_____

_____

_____

_____

We often live busy lives filled with current concerns and plans, so it's easy for life-altering experiences to eventually fade away. However, if we take the time to review those where we have no control over the outcome, yet He allows you to remain. Those experiences can be the light that helps someone around us get through the darkness. That's the power of testimony, as referred to in Revelation 12:11. After all, there's a reason why there are hundreds of verses in the Bible that emphasize the importance of remembering. Some of the text includes being ready to give an account, which is the modern-day equivalent of being prepared to tell somebody!

E.Y. Reflection
#7

16

IS JESUS CHRIST (INSERT RELIGIOUS PREFERENCE) R.P?

**For God so loved the world that He gave
His only Son, that whoever believes on Him
shall prosper and have everlasting life.
John 3:16 NKJV**

Key Points

1) The Jews misunderstood their role as special or chosen, when it really meant a special requirement.

2) Bigotry is a problem between us and God.

3) Any institution left to itself, primarily focused on its priorities, can become self-serving.

4) Don't put God in a box.

(Sermon Notes,
Oakwood Church, 2002)

My Reflection

Have you ever noticed the irony of how easy it can be for us to wear or use our religion as a badge, as if it gives us some form of glory? On another day (if we're lucky), proclaim and testify to the goodness of Jesus, yet keep all the benefits in-house. The reality is that it is God's goodness that is the only thing capable of making our filthy-rag-looking efforts seem beneficial.

All other attention gathering and chest puffing is truly a distraction to those actually interested in experiencing Jesus. If and when we get too caught up in religious pride and church politics or debating, it may be a good time to pray for God's help so that we don't become a stumbling block or point of distraction for those lost or troubled souls in search of a healing hand from their savior.

In the words of E.E. Cleveland, a humble, Southern-born, highly revered Christian evangelist and professor who led thousands annually to Christ by leading crusades. Fun fact (some of those programs were in partnership with Little Richard, a former classmate, no really, research that!) this took place around the world for 70+ years until his passing. While a professor at my school, Oakwood College (now, University) he would often say this pre-sermon prayer: "Hide me behind the cross so that I may never be so heavenly minded that I am of no earthly good" despite multiple experiences with Martin Luther King, Mandela, and one He famously called Lucy among others. But that's a story for another day. His words always intrigued me, ironically, as it seems that the closer you align your life with the Son of God, the more His light shines through. This results in an understanding of your weakness or dependence on Him. This is the polar opposite of being prone to feel more valued if you shared even a mere interaction with a "star" or one considered a celebrity.

As You Go...

Let's not be narrow-minded and think that our R.P (Religious

Preferences) are the only ones that will make it into heaven. We must not focus on why everyone else is not your R.P and concern ourselves with whether or not the spirit of God still abides by your R.P?

What three things can I change today that will make me more of an amplifier of Him than a distraction from Him?

What three things can I change today that will make me more of an amplifier of Him than a distraction from Him?

_____

_____

_____

_____

When your eyes become so narrow to the judgment of what others may have lacked. You may learn that the "everything" you thought was wrapped in your religion, there's one thing you left out. The vital link which is the love of Christ for His people regardless of their religious affiliation.

Someone asked a prophetess or religious author, Ellen White, if there was one single verse that could be used to bring a soul to God and what it would be, and instead of a doctrine-filled or fear-redden scripture, she offered John 3:16.

E.Y. Reflection
#8

Section IV

ON PURPOSE

17

TEMPORARY INCONVENIENCE FOR LONG TERM EFFECT (IMPROVEMENT)

**I can do all things through
Christ that strengthens me.
Phil 4:13 NKJV**

Listening to music is and probably will always be one of my favorite hobbies. For as long as I can remember music has been tied to fond memories. From my mom singing to watching aunts and uncle's flow and groove as instruments and vocalists let loose. While enjoying good music is okay we have to keep in mind what the Bible verse says about guarding the avenues of your soul. (Proverbs 4:23) One of my favorite genres is gospel. The quality of messaging in the lyrics, the variety along with the harmonies usually succeed in providing encouragement and a change of perspective to make getting through the day easier.

On rare occasions while listening to music, you get what I call a bonus blessing. I say 'bonus' because artists who have just a little more anointing will start ad-libbing, sharing things from their spirit. Typically, it comes in the form of a testimony, but every once in a while, it will just be the right combination of words or scripture that seem to be as impactful. I'll share one of the most notable memories. It occurred while listening to a Daryl Cooley album while working on a project. Towards the end of the already good song, he broke out with a testimony, which I don't recall word for word, but what stands out is his summary of how God impressed him in the situation. "It might be a temporary inconvenience, but it's for permanent improvement"

Oh, wow even now that almost makes me shout as it calls to mind that God always has a greater purpose and plan at work. How many times have you had either unfair or adverse situations arise that catch you off guard? Or have you ever felt like you were stuck in a season of continual misfortunes almost like you are being targeted? Well if you have rest assured I have a hand or two up with you. I'll share this one.

It was during one of my college summer breaks that I returned home from Alabama and was greeted by my mom and shopping partner who was excited to tell me about this new store with good clothes and AMAAAZING sales. Well, those are always welcome invites, especially since I had recently received my paycheck. Within a few days it was to the bank and to the store. We arrived at the shopping center but instead of going straight to the intended store the suggestion was made to just pop into the 99 cent store next door to pick up a few things. Now I don't know if you've ever been to that type of store that found some magical loophole in the system to offer like everything for the same price but, let's just say shopping quickly or with the "few things" rarely happened.

Despite everything, I went along. After all, every good shopping trip is made better with snacks. So with cash in hand, I went into the store and tried to slip the cash in my pocket. Unfortunately, I discovered I had no pockets and no purse, and for whatever reason, I didn't want to give it to Mom. So what did I do? My first thought was to roll it up and put it in my sock. However, on second thought, I opted for plan C, as I can't stand when things you put in there slide under your foot after you walk for a while. So there I was, browsing, catching deals, and throwing things in my basket, having a good old time.

As a plan C, the alternative was to place said money roll in the seam of my Swishy pants; as upon testing had a nice snug elastic hold on my waist. Swishy pants (break away sports gear popular late 90s that were perfect during the summer as it was breathable and light and made the swishing noise when you walked). So I moved around a bit, saw that the money was safe in its place so I continued on my way. Nearly a "quick "hour later with my cart in hand I got a rude awakening upon trying to checkout. Yep you guessed it, no money. I immediately went into panic mode scrutinizing every aisle I breezed down and to be honest even eyeballed a few people who came off sketchy but after ten minutes it was to no avail.

That situation still touches a nerve despite happening over 10 years ago, why do you ask? Let me let you in on the amount I lost $200 fresh from the bank dollars! That's a lot in general but for a college student at the beginning of her summer. Let's just say that a quick, bad decision affected me for weeks. Talk about a temporary inconvenience. I remember feeling various emotions from, "why is this happening to me? To maybe the other person needed it more despite none of those options managing to make me feel better.

I didn't get a random check in the mail to make me forget, but I learned more valuable life lessons that summer by being stuck with my thoughts and relying on prayer at home, since I didn't have money to go out. I was able to decide, as well as track contacts for post-graduation internships, and I got much-needed rest. When I returned to school the next semester, I even received a random $2,500 scholarship I never applied for, simply by showing up for my unofficial bi-monthly check-ins with my financial aid counselor. While the $200 loss kept me from looking at the gains as being 'worth it, I will praise God for making it work out (for your good despite) promise (Romans 8:28). I thank Him for keeping my mind through the tough times, which will inevitably return.

Not even for $10,000 would want to relive that situation. I will say, I'm more cautious on how I allow money to influence my wellbeing, and have grown to maintain a relationship with God even after it seems that He didn't answer what seems like an earnest, simple expectation to find the money. It's one of many experiences that enables me to become a valid witness that can tell you, Yes, while His ways may not be ours, He can and will ultimately work things out for THE good, like He promises. Seek Him and His way as I understand He has thousands of options that we have not even considered to bring about His will (E.G White) which may lead you in a better place than when you started.

As You Go...

When the bottom seems to fall completely out, do you leave enough room to search for options that He might have waiting in the wings?

_____

_____

_____

_____

How much value do you allow the temporary things of this world to take from the things that have permanent implications; like peace, love and perseverance?

_____

_____

_____

_____

E.Y. Reflection
#9

18

PURPOSE DRIVEN LIFE
I. Mitchell

Blessed is the man Who walks not in the counsel of the ungodly, Nor stands in the path of sinners, Nor sits in the seat of the scornful; But His Delight is in God....
Psalms 1 NKJV

1) We, should be what God wants us to be. Therefore WE should, not the other way around, where you seek to influence others on what you want them to be.

2) God's plans are eternal. Psalms 33:10-11.

3) The counsel of the Lord will stand. Proverbs 19:21

4) Testify! But when we do testify directly about God, not yourself.

    ... "Not according to our works. But according to His own purpose and grace." 2 Timothy 1:9, Isaiah 49:4

    If you want to be of use to God, get rightly related to Jesus Christ and He will make use of you unconsciously every minute you live-(My Utmost for His highest,) Oswald Chambers

(I. Mitchell, Sermon
Fifty Fourth St, 2007)

My Reflection

Can I testify! I'm usually not one to broadcast my entire life. But when you have that, "If I don't praise Him, the rocks will cry out for praise", with all of the life deliveries He's afforded. I, just can't miss the opportunity to praise Him when He performs a special thing.

I was nominated for a nationwide merit-based award by a good friend. And somehow, I was among the few people selected who received a Women in Business Leadership Award (Thanks, Apryl!). While that is an accomplishment I will appreciate for a long time, can I share from who? Ok, I can't hold it. The award will be coming from (my beloved) owners of 17 National Championships, home of Kobe Bryant, The Los Angeles Lakers. Yes, the very ones I may or may not ignore phone calls for while the games are on (over the last 20 years.) I was honored. Also so hyped! But also shocked.

I can go on about how it is a blessing to have been in the health promotion business for eleven going on twelve years; holding on through the rough times in some years when I've paid more than I made. Or spelling out some of the unexpected blessings of receiving free equipment and cool invites that turned into opportunities. But what is standing out for this little Black 80's baby in gang infested LA raised in a single-parent household. Is how this was even reasonably possible to get awarded at center court from her favorite team (one of the cities prized institutions). For context, L.A. celebrities constantly compete to pay 10k+ to sit front row, so when it was announced… It felt like a dream.

The notion gets more far-fetched when you consider that at the time I started JUSTMUV after being let go from my 1st real career job let go out of the blue in 2011. I didn't really have any other options. Well, since I had a lot of free time and was running out of money I figured that though the job was gone. The passion and skills God gave could be used to pursue interest and be impactful for others.

I am trying to tell you all "God is good", I have to say before I end this, growing up, my mom taught us that outreach is just what we do as God grants us life whether or not we deserve it. So with me and my siblings showing up for community has not required much thought to execute. At every turn, I knew it was the Lord who had been setting up little, "keep goings", it's really not about just your blessings.

As You Go...

When you consider your life, what fruit/ characteristic sparks your consistent ministry? (Don't forget to include whether or not you would ever receive a thank you for doing it options.)

_____

_____

_____

_____

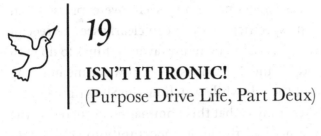

19

ISN'T IT IRONIC!
(Purpose Drive Life, Part Deux)

**Now to Him who is able to do
exceedingly abundantly above all that
we ask or think, according to the power
that works in us, to Him be glory in
the church by Christ Jesus....
Ephesians 3:20-21**

Yes, I know throwing in pop '90s songs is so cliché, but what better way to describe the series of blessings dipped in irony? For example, God's ability to keep my tank from empty while I offered a few more free events than I could afford. From the first payment I received coming in the form of an envelope with a $100 bill slid to me after a support group presentation. Talk. Admittedly, I was totally caught off guard, as my two goals where to get my feet wet & meet new people (Thanks Ron & Sheila). To receiving this award from a world-acclaimed company for a women leader in entrepreneurship for a regional best small business. The irony is that for many years, we typically provided at least 40% of our time to free outreach. Honestly, coming up with prices was a constant topic and a byproduct of many years of business counseling, as apparently, running a successful for profit business, without charging people is frowned upon.

The stress of the Lakers name may seem overexpressed, but let me share the specificity so you can clearly see the receipt for this God send. As a kid on of my favorite things to do with my late Grandpa (and 1st business coach) was time bonding while yelling at the refs while watching the Showtime Lakers on TV. Another irony is that this nomination occurred in the Pandemic, when I had the least opportunity to actually do business. I actually got the call a few weeks after I just paid for upgraded tickets (for the first time) after like ten years of being content to sit in the nosebleed seats. Then, not only would I be in the building for free, but that I will be in the building for free, I will receive an award mid-court and then be ushered back to the luxury box to watch the remainder of the game is accidental.

You cannot tell me that God did not set that thing up just so. What started as a concept in the mind as the last stretch grab for options to pay bills by helping people, has made room for me to be receiving an award center court, Jumbotron style! Hold mule! You can't tell me that my GOD IS NOT GOOD (and possibly has an appreciation for irony).

No, I'm not claiming this to be my last and greatest thing to accomplish, as I intend to continue pushing to create opportunities to impact others.

However, let me be a witness and share that if you put your plans before God. Give it what you have, ask for help, and remember, sure, while your skills are invaluable, that doing things for free periodically offers a sobering reminder that were called to impact ours instead just mine. Most importantly, just try it, and you will find that though it is not always going to be easy, you will learn more along the way as our perspective and opportunities can change with our position. You may find what you gained from moving would have never been found from staying in the same place with just your thoughts and doubts.

Support is crucial especially in hard times, so keep it close but if you ever need a cheerleader, if you can read this, you got me. I am not anyone special, but I think it's fair to say I know someone! Who can do Exceeding Abundantly, above all you ask or imagine. Ephesians 3:20-21

As You Go...

Sometimes, God alone knows how to use our strengths and weaknesses for His glory. Even more remarkably... to be real, it can be an annoyance sometimes when, despite much effort and activity, it translates into little if any progress. It can feel as if you were the only person in a waiting room and your name just will not be called.

It's a slow lesson to fully comprehend, but I'm learning that it's in those times that He is in the lab on your behalf. Maybe refining your character or trying to talk to you to clue you in on the next level you didn't know you were ready for. I Know! Frustration is hard, but if we can get to a place where we spend less time getting upset/ complaining or reacting; chances are we actually will have a clearer channel to receive the word from Him. A word that we were desperately standing in need of in the first place. Every now and again He'll reach into the unexpected and pour out an exceeding and abundant blessings to blow your mind. Even months after the experience, the what, how, and why still baffles my mind. However, I'm comforted, when I consider that God's thoughts and ways are higher than ours. Though

I may never know the why I'll settle with the words of one of my favorite Yolanda the Adams sayings referring to Gods movings:" Cause, He's just God like that."

How can you enhance your ability to use that more effectively for His glory?

_____

_____

_____

_____

E.Y. Reflection
#10

20

MISSION SCHOOL

For as we have many members in one body,
and all members have not the same office.
So we being many, are one body in Christ,
and every one member's one of another.
Romans 12:4-5 NKJV

Key points

1) Small parts are important especially if you are going downhill (think parts that make up a car).

2) The word used for gifts represents a divine grace in Greek.

3) We all bring many parts but contribute to one body.

4) Biblically, gifts are designated as different, with equal importance. They are to be used as a resource to benefit others.

Verse

For I say through the grace given unto me,
to every man who is among you, not to think
of himself more highly than he ought to
think, but to think soberly, as God hath dealt
to each the measure of faith. Romans 12:3

My Reflection

Generally speaking, it is widely held that the words talent and gifts are synonyms for each other. However, as Christians, our interpretation should change as the Bible draws a clear distinction between the two. I wonder if we considered whatever gift we excelled in from the standpoint of its ability to influence others. Would we be more inclined to hone and utilize them as opposed to holding them for safe-keeping?

The above text implies that mission is the objective behind the Lord extending His purgative to lend us talent. However, while it is ours to enjoy, practice, or share, we must be mindful that we also have the responsibility to develop, re-invest, and cultivate others with it. Ultimately, as with any other loan, the fee at some point will be due for repayment. The Bible is clear that to return it at the same rate is as unacceptable as letting it be wasted or underdeveloped (Matthew 25:25-26). For our sake and not only for the improvement of those in our growing sphere of influence, may the gifts of God's talents in us be multiplied into fruits that those in our neighborhoods and work places are grateful for, and not just those on your pew!

Verse

But now God has set the members, each one
of them, in the body just as He pleased.

1 Corinthians 12:18

Prayer

Lord, please grant me the courage, guidance,
and support to let the bonus light of Your gifts
shine through so that You may be glorified.

As You Go...

What are some of my natural talents?

_____

_____

_____

_____

Having natural talents costs nothing, so how could others
benefit from exposure if you chose to share them?

_____

_____

_____

_____

(Sermon Notes,
Madison Mission, 2003)

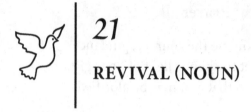

21

REVIVAL (NOUN)

To stimulate back into a lively state

L. Dorsey

Therefore gird up the loins of your mind, be sober, and rest your hope fully upon the grace that is to be brought to you at the revelation of Jesus Christ. As obedient children, not conforming yourselves to the former lusts as in your ignorance
1 Peter 1:13, 14 NKJV

Key Points

1) Dry bones characterize the conditions found in some churches' vitality. Referenced in Ezekiel 37:1. Most churches use organized business to replace the moving of the Holy Ghost.

2) Dry bones characteristics include being naked and scattered abroad, being idle and rebelling gratifying self, and perishing without fulfilling their duty to God.

3) The Holy Spirit can transform and bring new life. You can't catch the Spirit like a cold; it is an intelligible spirit, you must ask for it.

4) Attributes of the Holy Spirit are authenticity, good leadership, and love, according to John 16:13.

(Lawrence, Dorsey, Sermon notes,
Los Ángeles, 2001)

My Reflection

What does a Christian look like? I can almost guarantee that there is a different answer for every two, if not one, person who ever sat in any church on the planet, and at least two for those who never bothered to attend.

We could go on and on about what the proper attire is or when it should be put on, but rather than spinning our wheels in that quicksand, I feel a better concern should be: what impression do we leave behind?

Personally, I bounce between two thoughts on this one. On one hand, I feel that the true value of your Christianity should be measured by what or how you do things, far more than what an appearance can display. After all, actions speak louder than words, and anyone with money can buy nice-looking clothes, which has nothing to do with character. I once heard a saying when I was a teenager, and though I don't recall the person who quoted it, it was profound enough to stick with me to this day.

"The reason people have a hard time following others is that their actions are so loud that their voices are difficult to hear." –Author Unknown.

From time to time, my family and I visit a church that is primarily mixed with people who are not the same age, don't look the same, nor do they have musical tastes similar to those that we have generally enjoyed as a family. However, what keeps us returning to fellowship is the genuineness of their treatment of us from the day we initially stumbled upon that congregation. While there have been some ups and downs in the process, there is a unique beauty that comes from working through learning curves. As you come to understand perspectives of other cultures firsthand in attempts to grow together.

One event that occurred a few years back is a favorite memory with that group that brought the themes in the above sermon to life. During the holiday season, an idea was shared to have an outing for the Women's group. As the appointed date approached, several options were laid out. After several attempts to coordinate a viable plan, the group opted for less work to simply meet at a restaurant, so we went to Denny's. When the day came, a nice group of about 15 ladies of all ages and races and a few teens were in attendance. While managing to take up about 1/4th of the restaurant, we kept a respectable volume while sharing a few passages, having some laughs, and then exchanging gifts.

The food was great. Everyone enjoyed having waiters bring food on plates that did not need to be washed, and we had a good time catching up. When the plates were being cleared, we all began to work out the payment arrangement with those close to us in hopes of simplifying it for the nice waiter that day. Plans were finalized, and the waiter was called over. As the organizer started sharing the details and handing over the payment, imagine our surprise when the waiter refused our money. Happy but also confused, we asked a series of questions, and the waiter went further, explaining that it wasn't necessary as a guy paid for the entire table.

Hearing that brought even more joy, shock, appreciation, and even a few tears. Further questions on who and where the person was so that we could thank him revealed that the guy had left the restaurant already and wanted to remain anonymous.

Before that, he relayed to her that he was enjoying breakfast with his family. After watching our interactions, something about us impressed him, while he wasn't sure of the nature of the group, and he wanted to do something special. Not much beats great food than a gift of free great food and from a complete stranger! Wow, how random is that? Though our paths never crossed again, as far as I know, we said a prayer of blessing for him and his kindness. For the next few weeks, we all had a breakfast miracle story to tell to our families, not only for receiving free food but for God finding a way to use our fellowship and celebration in a public space to serve as a witness impacting unsuspecting onlookers.

Prayer

May our actions throughout the week (not only the weekend) be so aligned with His that we are living examples of God's character to those in our surroundings.

As You Go...

If the type of clothing or the look of a person weren't a factor, what are the elements that should be used to identify a Christian?

_____

_____

_____

_____

22

DOWN BUT NOT OUT
(300 CAR MONTY)

**And my speech and my preaching was not
with persuasive words of human wisdom, but
in demonstration of the Spirit and of power.**

**That your faith should not be in the
wisdom of men but in the power of God.**
1 Corinthians 2:4, 5 NKJV

Now we cannot...discover our failure to keep God's law except
by trying our very hardest (and then failing). Unless we really
try, whatever we say there will always be at the back of our
minds the idea that if we try harder next time we shall succeed
in being completely good...But in another sense it is not trying
that is ever going to bring us home. All this trying leads up to
the vital moment at which you turn to God and say, "You must
do this. I can't."

C.S. Lewis Mere Christianity;
Book III, Chapter 11 (excerpt)

My Reflection

If you've ever watched a movie based in a big city where a con
man or woman (let's be fair) needed to make a quick buck, then
chances are you've heard or rather seen the game Three Card
Monty! Just in case you have not, let me explain it to you.

Usually, the con artist will put a coin or mark, and etc., on a card. Three cards are turned upside down, and a person places a bet that you could not find the card that they have previously marked after they have been shuffled. As you can imagine, this often turns into an easy fundraiser as many times, the hand is quicker than the eye. Now, please don't turn this into your next get rich quick scheme, as the goal was an example to provide context for how God pulled out a modern-day miracle. Yet again!

Last year, I was so excited to join my family on an international destination wedding trip. We came out to soak in the smiles and millions of pictures for my nephew's wedding in Puerto Vallarta. As you can imagine the sites, food and all three wedding services were great, only accented by the fact that many of my family members were also there to enjoy it. What absolutely added to the magic was that I opted to spring some extra money on an all-inclusive hotel for the last day along with (but also on the other side of the hotel) that the bridal party was in, as I wanted to see what all the fuss was about.

If you've never tried it before it should definitely be on the list, as it is on the best travel decisions I've made in life list. This one had at least four restaurants, two smoothie and other bars were you can enjoy as much as you liked for free (after the hotel rate that is). So as a foodie you can be sure, I made it count even shared a few juice options with family while we waited in the hot sun between services (Bryan your welcome). Hmmm ok sorry that took me back to a happy place, let's get back to the story!

So on the last day I had two goals to accomplish after the lovely wedding (R and E 4ever!) before heading to the airport at about 3:00 pm. Reluctantly after eating my last meal and dragging checking out to the last 10 minutes I hailed a cab and spoke briefly with the nice concierge. I tipped him, threw my items in the cab and headed to stop by a few places to say goodbyes to family and friends then headed to the airport. Though the driver didn't speak a lot of English (granted we were in Mexico) I practiced the Spanish I knew and we had some good exchanges. He offered to take me to both places, so I wouldn't have to call for rides or wait twice.

I agreed and after the first drop off we headed to the second stop. On the way however, I got a call from my sister who wanted to also take the long ride across town to visit my dad and siblings who opted to go for a big rental despite it being 20 miles away. We opted to split the ride even though their rates were super low with most rides totaling like 70 pesos ($7). I informed my driver that the next stop would be the last instead of the original plan and when we got to my friend's hotel where my sister would meet me and I would join her cab. I asked the price and despite all of the Spanish he used he said $15 dollars. I paused and asked again, surprised for several reasons. For one every other person requested payment in their native Spanish, I thought maybe he was practicing his English and got the numbers turned about (as I'm sure I did talking to him) cause that is equal to 150 pesos for a 12 minute ride & nope! It seems as if he was trying to play me, So I asked why the price was so high and he went back into Spanish attempting to explain (ironically) so we stared bartering.

The other issue for me was that I only had 30 pesos left and a $10 and a $20 left over. Which sadly was too much and not enough. Despite the fact that he was overcharging me just the night before, a car full of my siblings rode clear across town on a 15-20 minute drive and paid only $8 or 80 pesos. Yet here I am (with no one else to advocate with me). Well he also shared that he took debit cards, which was an absolute NO, so after going back and forth we settled on my giving him $10 and 30 pesos which seemed to upset him. As he hurried me out the car, I was bothered because I was played and it was now about 1:00 pm meaning I would have to rush in order to do a short visit with the family and head 20 minutes back to make it back to the airport in the opposite direction by 3:00 pm.

I pulled it together and fought to keep all the negative Spanish words I knew to myself. I paid the guy and asked for him to open the trunk. I start to pull my things out and he rushes me then closes the trunk quickly gets in and drives off. While fuming mad at this point as I couldn't believe what just happened. I get out of the street and head up to say goodbye to my friend. After a short visit, my sister arrived to help me get my things and we jumped into the next Uber she had waiting. Still upset, I quietly stewed again and she joined me in being upset at the situation.

We got to my dad's and began our visit around 1:45 pm, hugged, ate a little food, and laughed with the house full of people. I shared that I only had a short time and would need to leave by 2:20 pm the latest to make it to the airport in time. They agreed and encouraged us to go on a walk to see the beautiful area and a huge surprise I just had to see. Now intrigued I accepted the offer but reminded them of my time constraints so they assured us we'd be back in 20 minutes tops. To move the story along, yes it was definitely worth it as the surprise was that there was a visiting exhibit of Egyptian huge tombs and other artifacts on display. After all the pictures and having a bonus of someone cutting down fresh coconuts for us to try.

I called the Uber to make my way and begin to gather my things. I went to where I laid my things, got my luggage and carry on but didn't see my jacket, so I asked those around about it and after three no's and a definite no you didn't come in with it I started to get nervous. By the time I heard someone ask if I was sure that I brought it I panicked as now it was 2:10 and the Uber ride was on its way and oh no I had to have left it somewhere! As they scanned the place I'm doing mental gymnastics trying to cross things off the list. My sister confirmed it wasn't in the car on the way, and I couldn't decide if it was at my friend's place. One thing was for sure, despite all of the people saying just to the airport you can get another jacket, it just wasn't that easy. I shared it wasn't possible and started planning to go back to the beautiful hotel where it first started. Now I know what you are thinking, girls just go to the airport, jackets not that important!

But does it change your answer that outside of it being a brand new Eddie Bauer frost resistant lightweight jacket. It was also my only work logo embellished coat that I should have never brought. Did, forget to mention that my car keys were in the pocket which I would need to drive myself home from the airport.

What are some of the things that stood out for you? Where would you have aborted the mission?

If this was a *Build Your Own Adventure* how do you think this ended? Based on your have experience, how do you think God showed up?

_____

_____

_____

_____

E.Y. Reflection
#11

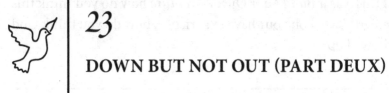

23

DOWN BUT NOT OUT (PART DEUX)

**The race is not given to the swift,
Nor the battle to the strong...
Ecclesiastes 9:12 NKJV**

So with high hopes, cluelessness, and a very distinct response from a family member that "there's no way you will get that back". I asked them to say a prayer with me and headed down for a ride. After sitting for a while I noticed the arrival time kept changing which is not at all what I needed at this point, I gave up on them and asked the attendant to call a cab 15 minutes later it came, and we were in our way around 2:30 pm again driving in the opposite direction of the airport on this *Where's Waldo* type mission praying that God would intercede. When getting back to the hotel I rushed to check the areas I last sat in, I saw my Amigo concierge friend who shouted "Back so soon? With a smile I told him what happened and inquired about the lost and found. Again after nothing appeared the hope of making the plane went down the drain. It dawned on me that maybe it was in the Taxi. Looking sad I sat trying to plan my next move, the concierge amigo came over to check on me so I told him that more than likely it was in the cab and since the guy is mad it's probably gone.

He asked if I knew which cab it was and of course I didn't, having seen hundreds since I arrived and with all the cabs in this vacation town of Puerto Vallarta it was a wrap, so I asked if he could call a Uber to the airport in hopes that maybe I can catch the next flight. He however asked a few strange questions like if I knew the driver's name and I think it was Jorge- which still left me at a loss as I'm pretty sure it's common around. He asked if he was tall or short, glasses?? I shared what I remembered and he said wait over there then he went to his booth. I didn't think much of it and as I was becoming defeated and resolved to take steps to arrange how I could get home from the airport back in California 10 minutes passed and the concierge came back with an update. I will never forget his words, he goes "I called the company Jorge already left work towards home but the boss is calling him back to drive here." My amigo said so much that at the time I couldn't piece the depth of all of it together. But when the part about him being on his way registered, I got extremely happy, thanked him profusely and asked how??? But he didn't answer but just gave a look as if to say, if he has the jacket, don't worry it will be in the car!

Now I'll never know what he said to the people on the phone but I imagine that it was Denzel Washington direct and exact because 10-15 minutes later guess who showed up. Jorge the Taxi cab and all after his work hours CLEARLY upset. Nonetheless he gets out of the car, my concierge hero meets him, they both exchange words and as they go to the back to the trunk he pulls out; guess what, My Jacket!!!

My now favorite amigo calls me over and says "you owe him money, can you give him $5 dollars?" (Which is now a total of 180 pesos). Though triggered, I was so shocked at all that happened that I didn't even protest, even though he gave me the stink face which was proof enough that he was holding my poor little jacket hostage. Before he left I checked the pocket and Yes! The keys were also there, my new best friend asked if it was ok, I nodded yes and he let the guy leave.

I thanked my hero again and he reminded me that I needed to leave. Yes he called a taxi cab over, which was thankfully still there, talked to them and gave me a "you go!" I put ALL of my things in the car and slid him more money and he gave me a thank you and he said see you again next time! Even till this day not only does how in the world that happened hit me and every family member that was surprised by my "look what God found" text message while on to the airport.

Well look at God! If anyone knows how to spot a jacket rolling around in one cab among at least 300 cabs in a 262.9 square mile city - wouldn't it be, the very one who knows the exact amount of hairs on each of our heads? He even worked out the plane situation so I could catch the first one leaving out in the morning at no additional cost, and that is exactly what I did. But this time I opted to rent a car having had enough of the middle men.

As You Go...

If ever there was a "With man it's impossible" but with God ALL (not some) things are possible (Matt 19:26) mustard seed situational experiment. I would be one of the million in the picture looking surprised but waving in the middle holding up a yep. He sure can sign. #whatamightyGodweserve!

Have you ever experience an impossible similar situation, if so how did God come through and did he also use other people to bring out this amazing feat?

_____

_____

_____

_____

E.Y. Reflection
#12

24

THE ORIGINAL HULK
J. Henderson
Referenced the story of Sampson

…So the woman bore a son and called his name Samson; and the child grew, and the Lord blessed him.
Judges 13: 1-25 NKJV

Key Points

1) During the bible era, judges were more like defenders or people on a rescue team. The story of Sampson is situated differently. For example, Sampson didn't get his strength until the spirit of the Lord came upon him.

2) The Philistines didn't know where his strength lied because he blended in with the crowd.

3) God wants us to be super people, where others look and are drawn by what we do that stands out and are themselves fascinated and want to know why.

(J. Henderson, Sermon Notes
Mt Rubidoux Church, 2011)

My Reflection

One of the questions the sermons brought to mind is: if we look, talk, act, and eat the same as everyone else, how could we convince others that we have something better to offer them? When you think of it that way, it makes you wonder if that is part of the reason why people don't find Christianity interesting or appealing. Yes, life is hard for us too. Yes, it can feel like an added responsibility to hold a smile in the midst of your situation, but it is what makes the difference. We know a God who is ready to shoulder whatever care we stand in need of. You know how I know??? Because He said He would.

There's a popular commercial that makes regular appearances on TV. Though I'm not going to use this as free ad space. The marketers use many attention-getting elements that make it hard to look away. The disclaimer is that the product does absolutely nothing beneficial for human consumption aside from accelerating death and wasting money. Despite having no desire to try the product, the narrator gives a list of death-defying challenges the survived, and seemingly impossible tasks that the person casually boasted about.

While the character is fictitious, I'm confident that whether you cared about the product you will know the spokesperson. Ok, say it with me. He is the most _____ man in the world! lol If you said interesting, give yourself a sticker as you got it right. Some may have thought of superman or some other larger-than-life character. Regardless, the fact remains that folks with great abilities, heroic stories, and even underdog triumphs at least garner attention and are positively influential and impactful.

These days, due to shifts in focus the ad hits a little differently. Now what comes to mind when the amazing list begins to roll are traits that have higher characters, are strong, have overcome through hard things, are courageous, and who planted them? Whether they were in my family or community, I am forever grateful that the Lord has blessed me with the ability to know and learn from them.

As You Go...

When you review elements in your life that looked more *Hulk*-like than incredible, which are a few that stand out the most?

_____

_____

_____

_____

25

HE THAT BEGAN A GOOD WORK! (PART DUO)

That the sharing of your faith may become effective by the acknowledgement of every good thing which is in you in Christ Jesus.

For we have great consolation in your love
Philemon 1:6-7 NKJV

We would be hard-pressed to find a Bible-reading Christian who could not finish the sentence in the title. Ironically, I was today old when I discovered that the verse had a point focus regarding remembrance preceding it. Perhaps that's a hidden gem. What if the valuable part of us being able to get to completion is in evaluating the blessing added to you, by people God allows around to be physical representations to sojourn and support?

Across the course of my journey so far, springs of blessing have overwhelmingly at times flowed from supportive women along with my mother (of course). There have been some Pearls, Sam's, Essie's, Shenay's, Dena's, Sali's, Elaines, Shannon's, Shelia's, Sherrys a Lex and Sistah friends (sooo many S's.) Their influence spills over into my pay it forwards and are worth their weight in gold. While I make no apologies for their inclusion in this book. The hope is that it also brings to mind people significant to your support system as well! I can't name them all. But trust that I have asked that God will repay them in abundance, along with many other relentless ones in my family that God has allowed in my life. They all tend to know how I feel, so this time I feel compelled to change it up and shine the light on a few good men that have also made an impact. I might even revel in it just a bit more, as they each have an ironic preference for remaining in the background.

Exhibit A

They called him Bob. He was a man's man and rarely wasted words, as for him, a better use of energy is to commit the effort and get to the results. Often forgoing motivational speeches for after-work flights to the capital to advocate for union workers rights. He shared long love letters and promises in 59 years of marriage, and only a handful of missed team games or performances between nine grandkids across four cities. People easily gravitated to him as he was well versed and seemed to always have a step-by-step response for how to get from, what you thought was a good idea at the time, to what the most effective steps were to materialize the goal you wanted to achieve.

For me, it was starting a business, but that gift could even be felt in everyday life, with people in need of help with directions to get from one city to another without the freeway in hopes of avoiding traffic. He would ask for the street you were on and maybe what was around you, and he would provide turn-by-turn options long before GPS. Those years as a cab driver really paid off! He had more military than college experience before the GI bill inspired jobs to respect or accept it. That lit a never-say-die fire strengthened by God's grace and determination, resulting in at least three successful startup businesses.

Leading to 40+ years of self-made career securing a legacy for his six kids, contributing to at least 10 college degrees, and casual conversations that he had with greats like Elvis, Ella Fitzgerald, and many commendations from state reps, and until his death, yet he rarely missed regular family dinners. Not too shabby for a little Black boy thrown into the WWII draft fresh out of high school from a segregated town so small you would have a hard time finding it on a map of Louisiana.

They called him Bob, and I was blessed to call him Grandpa. Talk about a Jeremiah 29:11 "I know the plans I have for you" testimony. From him, I learned to count on God. That excuses don't exist. That the Lakers are a family team, and jazz is the best type of music.

Exhibit B

His name is common, though some would say it's a little dated, as it's rare to even hear it in passing these days. The value of his pretty much volunteer godfather-like presence for me and my brothers since childhood has been priceless.

While the consistent words of support and celebration cards are always stuffed with surprises, they usually come at the right time. No amount of the things can outweigh being introduced to others and treated as family, complete with open door policies, and getting aunt's, uncles and cousins who have done the same for the last 30+ years. No one on this side of the ground is without flaws, but as time has gone on, flowers are more enjoyable when they can be smelled.

I can't put the full influence and impact in a nutshell, so I share a situation that recently happened on a random day last year when I decided to visit as I was close to his city. It had been a while, and there was a Christmas gift I wanted to drop off. Though I called only five minutes away, we soaked up the game, and I was invited to stay for a homemade steak dinner with the family. We chatted a bit, and I thanked them and started for home. When I was about five miles away, he called because I left something and also because he forgot to give me my birthday present (two months prior). I was tired; it was late, and I had a long ride, so I shared that I'm on the way to the gas station and that I could pick it up next time.

What happened next still blows my mind, as without a hitch, where are you? I gave the street names; he said to turn left and you will see a Shell station two miles away. Go there, and I'll meet you there shortly.

It felt like I had no choice in the matter, so I did just that. He pulled up, pointed me to the open gas pump, and brought the things I left. I turned to put them in the car, and he had already swiped his card and started pumping gas. I was shocked. Smiling, I begin to thank him; he brushes over it with a sure, "I missed your birthday, so don't worry about it." As the conversation continued, so did the price, and after attempting to politely dissuade him, I shared that half a tank should get me home. When that was shot down. I went back to my lane of answering questions and chatting, and then the sound of the full tank clicked. Smiling ear to ear, I hugged and thanked him again profusely, and by the way, I have a mid-sized SUV that was just above EMPTY in California. He smiled, said you're welcome, and told me to drive safely. He said hi to my mom, watched me drive off, then left. Who does that?? Someone clearly connected to Jesus. His name is Walter, and the verse that often comes to mind when I think about his influence is "every good and (even not-quite) perfect gift is a necessary gift from God (reminding you that He cares)" (James 1:17). My amplified translation.

Exhibit C

Though shouting was his preferred means of communicating, maintaining an outwardly cranky nature was high on the list of things you initially noticed about him. My introduction to him was by someone close to the family: "He's the coach that yells all the time, but you'll love him!" While annoyed at how presumptuous and basically dismissive they were. It turns out that it usually takes about two exposures to learn that it really was the love language of one of the most beloved faculty members at Oakwood University, my Alma Mater.

Whether headed to the gym for a class or passing by, you would readily hear his voice shouting out instructions or engaging with a former student who would stop by. Despite his volume, his forward movement & consistency told another story, often making time to interact with students regardless office hours and personal attention to not only keep the sporting facilities in working order but frequently be found leveling and chalking the softball fields before games, even though the school had a perfectly capable landscaping team, All of this completely contradicts the crabby coach vibe, especially as most of this occurred after a full day of work. The word abnormal, at the very least, could be a good way to describe him.

Given all the grizzly actions that took place in the Deep South during the civil rights movement, I guarantee the impact no one saw coming would be one connected to his story. So, what happens when a White American male feels it is his calling to seek a job at a HBCU in Alabama? Well, a beloved teacher of 50+ years. He also basically led the development of Oakwood's athletic department. Hundreds of students were welcomed to home-cooked meals and weekend worship with his family.

That stat is surpassed by the thousands donated by him or as a direct result of a call to now prosperous former houseguests. Those funds have bridged the tuition gaps to allow kids to stay in school or maintain recreation availability so students would have a healthy on-campus outlet. We were all saddened by his sudden passing a few years ago, but thankfully, he left six actual children with the same tenacity and worldview. Add that to generations of students who still light up and are eager to share a story of a selfless, funny, or principled act they witnessed. His name was James Roddy, or "Coach Roddy" the guy whose favorite word had to be dagnabbit! As he often used it as a noun adjective and verb. I and hundreds were blessed to call him coach. If pledges and building plans go as promised by Oakwood's administration, a new state-of-the-art gymnasium will be completed and named in his honor, ensuring countless others will remain exposed to his unique, dedicated, Christ lead legacy.

As You Go…

Throughout the list of circumstances and family dynamics, I grew up around at times required more gymnastics than just dynamics to maintain balance. Like the unexpected passing of close family members, juggling inconsistent behaviors of loved ones, and making things fun. Growing up in the 80's in the middle of Los Angeles, to name a few. But I'm so glad that God mapped out what I needed before I even arrived. It's as if he poured in stabilizing doses of people disguised as blessings and even an older brother who I may not understand until I'm over 50 (it is a common condition the siblings have I'm told) lets call him B. He does invaluable things like lending me his new pc throughout my master's program. Eventhough he may be the last person to answer my calls, he's the same one that would let me pay him back then gifted me the same PC as a graduation gift. God makes timely substitutions to support the promises of his covering grace.

He also saw fit to add in a pray first and always mother as a door-buster deal. Joel 2:25–26 shares this promise: "And I will restore to you the years that the locust hath eaten... And ye shall eat in plenty, and be satisfied, and praise the name of the Lord your God that hath dealt wondrously with you"...

How would you characterize the type of provision God has allow in your life?

_____

_____

_____

_____

What or who could you point to as significant additions that made that journey easier to walk through?

_____

_____

_____

_____

E.Y. Reflection
#13

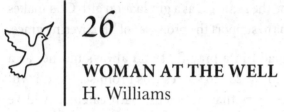

26

WOMAN AT THE WELL
H. Williams

> And at this point His disciples came, and
> they marveled that He talked with a woman;
> yet no one said, What do you seek? or,
>
> Why are You talking with her?"
> **John 4:27 NKJV**

1) The Rubinicle Rule prevented men from talking to women in ancient times.

2) In Genesis 2:23 Jesus was trying to teach us the significance of how, through Christ, women are to be restored to an equal position.

3) In John 4:29 the use of "come see a man" is an important approach to introducing Christ as it allows people to have their personal experience for self-discovery.

4) Sometimes, when we are too familiar with Jesus, it causes us to also be more concerned with the physical instead of the spiritual. As it seemed that the disciples were primarily focused on the woman He talked to as opposed to what they talked about.

5) We can sometimes have so much spiritual food, but do we do enough to share it?

(H. Williams,
Loma Linda, CA, 2009)

116

While it's clear that Christ was interested in helping the woman, it is also apparent that He, in His infinite wisdom, was using this experience to teach a profound lesson that has surpassed time and remains for the benefit of all of us. Whether it is how to not let man-made traditions stand in the way of opportunities for spiritual restoration or another example of Christ humbling or refocusing His disciples on the fact that He is God and not limited by other people's expectations. We, at the very least, can have an example or embodiment of how to be so desperate in your pursuit of Christ that you are undeterred. Undeterred by your pride and the criticism of religious leaders, stand ready and willing to exchange all that He has to offer for whatever heavy weight you can seem to shake, even at a chance encounter at the water cooler.

As You Go...

The message shared was so rich that in this passage I felt no need to add my reflection.

Outside of Christ in this message, can any one of us also extend to others the same opportunities offered at a present-day "well" experience? Why not?

_____

_____

_____

_____

If so, in this modern day age, how would extending the "Well" experience look?

_____

_____

_____

_____

Section V

CLOUD OF WITNESS

Since we are surrounded by so great a
cloud of witnesses, let us lay aside every
weight, and the sin which so easily ensnares
us, and let us run with endurance the
race that is set before us Hebrews 12:1

27

THE BEAR
B. Young

> No temptation has overtaken you except
> such as is common to man; But God is
> faithful; who will not allow you be tempted
> beyond what you are able, but with the
> temptation will also make a way out of
> escape, that you may be able to bear it.
> **1 Cornthians 10:13 NKJV**

Homophones! Not sure if you have heard of it before but in addition to being on the list of my favorite words to say, the meaning offers just another reason to be cool. They represent words that sound the exact same but has varying meanings. For example-plane and plain which each have about four meanings, interesting right! While your brain is probably downloading all the other ones. Because my curiosity usually runs away when I have to stop and wonder if the Bible is using a homophone for our verse. As we have gone through challenges, which really cause us to wonder which description most accurately reveals the weighted load; that is allowed to signal the call needed for divine intervention.

I'll tag my mom to describe what she refers to it as one of the most difficult times in her life; despite moving from trial to triumph on the other side of MANY other personal, career or family changes. I'll let you be the judge on if this circumstance was the <u>Bear</u>- with grizzly characteristics and ferocity with intensity greater than lions, tigers … Oh My! (Yes, I had to do it) Or would it be the <u>Bare</u> that sends more vibes of a person continually receiving items attempting to navigate it?

Whether asked for or not, these are given past their ability to hold or handle the weight without it causing the loss of balance; leading to a fall physically but also spiritually. So here it is. While juggling single parenting three kids, two of which were teens in LA in the 90's. My mom lost four loved ones in four months. That list included, her mother, brother, sister and a close friend who ironically was often a prayer partner. Anyone would need a good month to recover from the loss of a good neighbor, but four immediate family, all from unrelated situations. Lord?! This is how she shared her experience. (Tag Mom, you're it)

"What stands out for me is just how good God truly is: He brought me through the loss of my mother to a stroke in October; loss of my brother of lung cancer in Nov. Loss a dear friend in January of diabetes and my sister with a brain aneurysm in February of 1999. I almost fell apart with grief. It was so overwhelming. I felt like I was on automatic pilot! Drifting through chores and duties of the day as I still had responsibilities; but was disconnected, lost, sad, all cried out, and drained. I continued to go to church. I heard encouraging words, prayers of comfort, and helpful visits.

As You Go…

Several thoughts and scriptures came to mind like, Phil 4:13, I can do all things through Christ, who strengthens me. Also, do not fear or be dismayed for I'm your God…I will strengthen you, Yes I will help you, I will uphold you with my righteous right hand. Amen! Isaiah 41:10. I held and <u>still hold</u> these and other scriptures in my heart; they humble and give me peace.

Time has also helps to heal through the trials of life, listening to encouraging music like my favorite song never would have made it by Marvin Sapp provides a welcome source reinforcement to hold on to God as He is truly the only one who could have brought me through.

When you recall the times that you can be considered your "worst days" even if you can't recall all the ins and outs, what elements about getting through do you remember? Can you share if there were key people or things that were said that gave you strength to go on?

_____

_____

_____

_____

E.Y. and B.Y.
Reflection #14

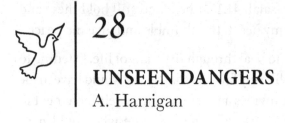

28

UNSEEN DANGERS
A. Harrigan

**"He will keep you safe from all hidden dangers and from all deadly diseases."
Psalms 91:3 GNT**

When we pray, we often thank God for protection from seen and unseen dangers. Most often we don't even think about what those dangers might have been. I have found that it is not until one is face to face with that danger that true appreciation of God's protection is found.

Sitting in a hospital waiting room, praying, and waiting for the doctor to update me on my husband's surgery, I was beyond stressed. The procedure to remove his gallbladder and appendix was supposed to be two and a half hours from start to finish. However, as I stared nervously at the clock noting that it had been four hours since they started, I realized something must have gone wrong. Frantically I called the nurse in the post-op area and asked for an update. "The surgeon is not finished yet," she said. "But he'll come out and talk to you when they're finished." Trying to calm down and focus on something positive I sat down, prayed, and listened to one of my favorite podcasts. After another hour, which seemed like an eternity, the doctor finally came out to speak with me. Shaking his head he said, "It was really, really bad. What normally takes me 20 minutes took 3 hours! Your husband had so much tissue damage in there, I'm surprised he wasn't in pain long before this." Shocked and overwhelmed with this news, I didn't know what to think or feel. I was relieved that my husband had survived this emergent surgery but fearful of what could have been

Two weeks later, during my husband's follow up with the surgeon, he was able to convey to my husband the severity of his prior condition. His gallbladder had basically died inside him and was infecting the surrounding tissues. Additionally, his appendix was on the brink of rupture. He mentioned that only 2% of the people he's seen with similar cases have survived with this type of condition. Upon hearing this, a flood of emotions erupted in both my husband and me. With tears in our eyes, we couldn't help but be filled with overwhelming gratitude to God for saving my husband's life. We had no idea the dangers that we were living with on a daily basis, but God in His love protected my husband.

As You Go...

Are you aware of some unseen dangers that God has protected you from?

_____

_____

_____

_____

How has that affected your faith?

_____

_____

_____

_____

Given, what you've learned after making it through any of those situations, would you change anything about it? If so, what would it be?

_____

_____

_____

_____

(Testimony by
A. Harrigan, 2023)

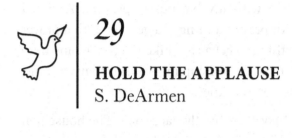

29

HOLD THE APPLAUSE
S. DeArmen

Do not be overly righteous,
Nor be overly wise:

Why should you destroy yourself
Eccl 7:16 NKJV

Ever since I was a little girl I loved to pray and loved Jesus. Beats me how words leaked out amongst the good saints that I could get a prayer through, but there they came, lined up with their prayer request. Like dear, sweet sister B. without fail, every week would say "I know you're praying for me, right Staci!" c'mon now. I got a date with Tom & Jerry at 2:00 pm, snack time with Dick & Jane at 3:00 pm and a game of "doctor" with your grandson at 4:00 pm. But instead, I'd shoot up a quickie prayer before we'd meet, so it would feel like I would not go to hell for lying. "Yes sister B., I prayed for you."

Then there was a sister lady at my church requesting to see *me* so I could pray for her before the ambulance whisked her away. I'd never even met her. I was more into Clearasil & Debarge. I guess word got out. She died a few hours later. *I could have saved her!* If only I'd arrived just a few minutes earlier.

Once I'd been around the block a few times, it was now time to step up my game. I wanted to pray prophetically like the cool cats. I'll tell you your future, your past & everything in between. Hot dog! This was getting good! I was getting better.

I'd razzle-dazzle 'em with my big public prayers. And if I couldn't get 'em with prayer coming. I'd get' em with a prayer request going! Anything to get a rise. Like the sun. Come unto me. I'll pray for you. Come worship me. I mean *pray* with me. Let us pray, together, on our knees.

Then last year, on May 18, it finally happened. The house that Staci built (to myself) cracked straight down the middle to its very foundation.

My pastor preached a sermon based on Eccl 7:16 "Be not righteous over much; neither make thyself over-wise why shouldest thou destroy thyself"

Uh-oh. Uh-oh. Getting close to home. He's talking to me & about me. He's putting my business out there in the streets. Help me, Jesus!! This was some modern-day Balaam craziness. (Numbers 22:5-7) "I came to myself" and for the last year, God has been returning me to myself over & over again. You see, prayer has become my idol. I might not have good health, any money, or many friends. but I could pray my behind off, big deal.

So with my cards on the table I took close inventory of how my close friend M., prayed & Ms B. Both humble, devout women of God who claimed the promises of the Bible- not like the ooh, wee, front row seat, packed house prayers I would pray, minus one solitary promise. Weak, limp, lazy prayers. God Forgive Me! And He did! With open arms. As in the prodigal son story "but when he was still a great way off, his father saw him, had compassion, and ran and fell on his neck and kissed him." Luke 15:20

And so, with no tricks up my sleeve, I prayed to God without trying to impress the listener. I pray His beautiful promises with quivering lips & trembling soul knowing He's really, really listening. I pray to my Holy Father. The King of kings & Lord of lords with no applause necessary.

(Testimony by
S, DeArman,2022)

Section VI

POETIC RECUPERATION

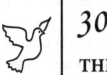

30

THE PARABLE OF THE SPIDER
(True Crimes 2011 Ed.)

Now you won't find this one in the Bible,
but when the Lord uses the little things to
teach great lessons it bears repeating.

While I can't say that a donkey gave me orders or I had an ant to give me a mini sermon, the Lord did something pretty amazing with a spider. The other morning I found myself struggling to wake up for work, as I had a long night the day before. So after pressing the snooze button a few times to no avail, I prayed that the Lord would help me to make it work (I just started a new assignment at work, you know how that goes).

Soon after, my eyes opened up enough to notice something in my peripheral that did seem right. When I sat up I found that no more than a foot from my head was a spider (I live outside of the city so don't judge me). Immediately, I jumped clear out of bed and cleared whatever was in my way. Needless to say, in addition to being alive I made it out of my house and to work earlier than I had in a long time, I learned that day that coffee is nothing compared to adrenaline.). God is soooo awesome!!!

See what's amazing (I don't want you to miss it) is that what God does is so confounding that it made me realize that, sometimes we miss out on what the Lord is trying to do in our lives because he sometimes uses things that are bad situations to get in a place that we need to be. It touched me so deeply because I HATE Spiders and if it would have been an ant or some other thing I wouldn't have the same testimony Now some might pass it off as coincidence but it's not how I see it. My pastor recently preached here and he spoke about how having a vision is so beneficial because, by having it you can begin to open your eyes to the opportunities that are around you; that will get you to that destination that sight alone could not(paraphrased). Though he was referring to vision I believe the same is true in this situation. I would rather know that God has an expected end for us and therefore look for His daily moving in my life, then to miss out heavenly options with the consolation of random selection.

E.Y. Reflection
#15

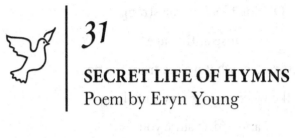

31

SECRET LIFE OF HYMNS
Poem by Eryn Young

We start with the Jesus Love hymn
and shouts as we praise Him

Then after years of rote memorization

But at a slow cadence it begins
to retract our motivation

Mom whyyyyy is this blue book do heavy...

⁻(Dragging) Softly and
Tenderly Jesus is waiting

Calling for yooooou and for meeeeee!⁻

Mmm maybe if the call was rhythmic and loud

More people would answer!

Sermon preached wait... nope,
that was a speech I bet I can guess
what song she's gonna sing...

Yep, come to Jesus was the plea

Great now can we go eat!

Then on to next week

When were back for a shampoo, rinse & repeat

Oh don't look at me strange

Cause at that age

We just reflect what we see from the pews

Like when a song was quite long

and didn't suite you

Your distain really did shine through

and shortly after our minds followed too

As I got older life trials grew bolder and
Comfort started leaving in phases

Then words that we would sing
start taking new meaning

And those memories turned into my blessings.

Pass me not gets requested

and those problems you came with
fall off when you praise Him.

As refreshing seems to leap off the pages

See before Marvin ever could have made it

Or Kirk would have tried to
sing it or change it.

Folks like Fannie Crosby, El Nathan

and Bev Shae

Pushed through their burden
and sought prayer

Out of their despair, penned songs
that helped them to freedom

Even now just by their songs

Rhyme attached to meaning

With pass me not, showers of blessings

And we can't forget I'd rather have Jesus

When blindness kept Fannie from seeing it

By faith she conceived it

Writing all the way my savior leads me

See here is the secret

Over coming trials is what breeds hymns.

Then when praise teams decide to sing them

Anthem they conjure chill as their original
feelings get rebirthed through singing

Now my testimony in the bank

when my only option

Was to duck and hold the truth of my life
read like the refrain from He hideth my soul

As bullets and shouts rang out and I know
I had been hid in the cleft of the rock

Had He not taken me their

I truly could not be here!

ˉHe hideth my life in the depths of His love

and covers Me there with His handsˉ

That's why without Hymn I am null

ˉAnd covers me there with His handˉ

E.Y. Reflection
#16

Deliverance Haiku

Like phone off charger
I stand waiting for reception
Beep Beep, pressed, held, home

Section VII

A LITTLE EXTRA

**For those days when it seems that
circumstances look like more than you can
bear, than the strength you have to offer**

*32

STONES FROM AN UNLIKELY BED
K. Paschal

> … It came to pass that the Lord spoke
> to Joshua the son of Nun, Moses
> assistant, saying:…Arise, go over the
> Jordan, you and all this people…
> Joshua 4: 1-24 NKJV

Key Points

1) In Joshua 4:7 God instructed Joshua to take the Israelites through the Jordan, without revealing all the details for how to cross. Research even suggested that this occurred at a part of the season when the river was at its highest point during the year. Sometimes God waits until circumstances are so great that you will have no doubt who it is that has brought you through them.

2) Sometimes there are mountains that He'll bring to you to climb and then drill a hole there where the only way you could make it would be to crawl through. Other times He will give you the ability to climb. So we know God is good because it is him that was our destiny all along!

3) Verse 21 Gave specific instructions to bring a stone back so that when their kids asked about them, they could give their testimony on how God did not allow

even their feet to get wet. Recalling that it occurred in the season where the waters were the highest. This is a message for us even now as it would be an ever-flowing blessing for generations if we keep reminders around that can keep us ready to testify of how God without a shadow of doubt saved you.

4) The scars that you have on your on your body is a testament to the mercy and grace of God that brought you through. So don't try to tell them about how tough you are! Tell them how God brought you through!

(K, Paschal, Sermon notes
The Pastors Pulpit, 2021)

My Reflection

There are many descriptions Christ used in scripture to characterize himself, however Alpha and Omega seems to be the most complete. Everything about this thought called my attention to the thoroughness at play with this project, much so that the best way I can explain it other than serendipity is intentional. The divine irony involved with this message happened that there was no choice but to split the placement of this not infrequently used but poignant story in two spots for this book. I'll use the same terms in hopes that I will paint a better picture. For context I'll start with the Alpha or background of how this project began. This writing journey started in 2021 right in the middle of the Covid pandemic. During that time we were in a season of finding ways to figure out how to cope with being locked down, and the prospect of returning to work was a far fetch option as I worked for the school district and the kids and their family had to be kept safe along with the elderly.

After attempting new forms of distractions e.g. hobbies I soon grew board of puzzling, online meetups to replace actual excuses to socialize. To break the monotony I picked up a pen and started brushing up sermon notes that was rushed through and unclear then decided that I would at least enter them for posterity since I had so much free time. However while reviewing the words from various sermons fifteen year prior would begin to touch my heart prompting me to include some elements of testimonies about Gods continuing to come to my rescue which were next added to amplify the parts of the given message.

Throughout the process I have had several starts and stops due to shifts of creative energy that came along with the added stress of losing loved ones (with as many as 6 non Covid related deaths in the family in one year), beginning new jobs responding to family illness and even uncertainties from catching Covid myself. So to say God has been a stabilizing force for sanity and health would be an understatement!

In one of my low capacity to write stages in 2022 I ran into my high school religion teacher at a local event, even though he and his family reside on the East Coast. After some time was spent catching up and also taking pictures I decided I'd share with him info about this devotional, after all who wouldn't want reasons to lets some of your favorites feel a little pride in the continuation of habits that they inspired you towards. I explained some dilemmas I was experiencing in working on the project and asked if he wouldn't mind reviewing it and offering his thoughts as many years as one of his students established the wisdom of his opinion as it matched his character. The fact that he has over 40 year of experience pastoring didn't hurt the cause either as I figured a trained pair of eyes could only enhance the spiritual soundness. He agreed to check it out and offered a wealth of incite as well as revision not only once, which was a labor of love to do since he lived across several time zones, but continued to extend the kindness several other times refusing to accept my payment for time offered(Mr, P. Thanks again).

Fast forward to 2024, where I had completed 80% of the book thanks to many friends and family members who I've polled on everything from title ideas to second and third opinions on story choices for what has moved from my initial plan for a 30 day offering to one that kept growing. Along the process, I made it a point to check in with God on the direction of the project as self-established deadlines began to approach and pass having not received a word from the Lord otherwise.

Now on to the Omega and clear sign to wrap it. On Saturday morning I was awakened around 7:30 which was considerably early for me as I had been up writing until 2am the night before and even set my alarm to rise at 915 to help compensate for that... Once awake I did a few safety checks and noticed no danger so I prayed the returned to a comfortable position hoping to just go back to sleep but that was of no avail.

At that point, I thought that I should just go back to writing since sleeping was no longer an option but as I attempted to pick up where I left off in hopes that I could have that story complete before it was time to go to church. I opened the screen but the wheels just would not roll. Again with plenty of time to kill I started brainstorming on ways to thank my bible teacher for his help on the project and the thought came to me to find a way to include him in this book as a thank you. After going through several piles of notes I could not find one from a live sermon I already used as a reference point (similar to the other key points used in this devotional).

It dawned on me that, the best I could do at this point was to browse online, watch and let the spirit move me into what needed to be shared. I came across at least a dozen on the site and since none in particular stood out I clicked one randomly vowing that if it didn't grab me I could just select another. What happened next I couldn't make up if I tried, perhaps from our mouth to God ears is a real thing? From the time the video started until I ran out of space writing notes on the above message the message fit the breath of this project like a glove.

With the same Divine irony that pops up right on times found a way to make yet another special appearance. Here are several elements involved allowing a clear sign to this being the very one I needed to complete the project even though the message originally aired in 2021.

1) I'm rarely productive before 8am. Also, the only time I wake up that early on a weekend is if I am or a family member sick/in an emergency or I am traveling.

2) Though initially unfamiliar with the story about Joshua and the tribe in Bible it struck the first cord on learning that river they've been told to cross didn't part for them until their foot stepped in. To which he shared that there will be trials you will have to go through in life that are so difficult, that your survival will be a clear indication that it was God who could have got you through... Funny having many close calls is the basis of this book.

3) The second cord was him sharing a testimony of how God created a special delivery for him and his siblings... Interesting three of the eight deliveries in my life story also involved surviving car accidents

4) For cord three at this point you've gotten so far in this books journey that All I should have to say is, THE STONES! before a good praise or at least a thank you shout should drop!...Refer to point 3 of the sermon again if you missed it. And so I'm adding it as the last message even though the messaging also serves as a preamble and the finale.

As You Go...

The more I get into the word of God the more I am coming to understand how we can never comprehend the Sovereignty aspect of God. That was more than enough confirmation for me to know that none of this effort would be in vain if anyone in my legacy or where ever they only stumble over this stone creating the opportunity to recount Gods marvelous works. Despite it all, He helped me to make it through. Now I can testify that the pains and the uncertainties associated with delivery was well worth it!

Did you find something impactful in this message? If so, what stood out and why?

_____

_____

_____

_____

Scriptural References by Title

Scriptural References by Title

Scripture	Title	Page
Philemon 4:13	Temporary Inconvenience...	77
Psalms 51	Purpose Driven Life	82
Ephesians 3:20-21	Isn't it Ironic!	85
Romans 12:4-5	Mission School	89
1 Peter 1:13-14	Revival!	92
1 Corinthians 32:4-5	300 Car Monty	96
Ecclesiastes 9:12	Down but ...(Part Deux)	102
Judges 13: 1-25	Original Hulk	106
Philemon 1:6-7	He That Began	109
John 4:27	Woman at the Well	116
1 Corinthians 10:13	The Bear	121
Psalms 91:3	Unforeseen Dangers	124
Ecclesiastics 7:16	Hold the Applause	127
----	The Parable of the Spider	133
Hymn- He Hideth...	Secret Life of Hymns	135
Joshua 4: 1-24	Stones from an Unlikely...	141

Acknowledgements

I started this journey with *Its Kinda Funny But... Jesus Saves* as the title and while the road through life can feel that way, this writing process has change my perspective. With that, I thought and upgrade in title more focused on highlighting Gods working vs calling attention to my side of the road would by more fitting.

Thank you for taking this journey with me, I'm confident that you may be able to more easily recognize the blessing of receiving *Special Deliveries* by the hand of God. Ill also; like to thank all who have had a part in pulling this together, from my second opinions-ers, editors, prayers, and even the those whose sermons I enjoyed all those years back. I may have only tipped the iceberg of your message with this book to pass long to keep that blessings rolling going forward, but I was careful to include the location so by all means if you are looking for a solid church to attend google their names any of theirs would be perfect. Now that you've taken a peak at the Beautiful/ Ironic/ Atypical way the Lord reveals lessons to me, perhaps you will consider and pray about what Divine Ironies or Special Deliveries "happened" to follow your walk.

You never know, your book will be the next jewel that inspires another person to cling to God and keep pressing on through the adversities that attempt to disturb us from living the abundant life He intended for us.

(When you do message me (IG @Eyoungspeaks2) I'd love to read it! Hopefully the writing prompts have helped.)

Reviews

I liked the short quotes/stories that you have at the top of each chapter. They help draw the reader in. You have a great writing enthusiasm that helps each story come to life. I literally saw the trapped squirrel in my head! I felt the tension in the basketball team and the dude trying to holla situation. I sensed the hope and stress that you experienced in that situation-ship. As always, you have a way of telling a story like no other. -*JeNean Lendor*, Editor's note

I loved the story on God turning around the madness of losing $200 in being blessed with a scholarship you never applied for! I know the book will touch many who still have time as it reached me & I'm an older one. -*Ms Essie Brown*

Eryn Young does a fantastic job of relating biblical stories to everyday life situations. You definitely want to read this book if you desire to seek the connection between the biblical hero's in the Bible and how that relates to you. -*Marilyn Dunn*

The miracles in your life have been huge! I have similar testimonies. You have a great writing presence. The stories are true miracles! Great idea to share. -*Ms Sali Butler*

Eryn weaves a compelling story of God's grace and mercy by highlighting the angels who have carried her along the way. Her testimonies are unbelievable, unless you have your own lived experience with the God of the impossible. You will encounter Jesus The Savior within these pages in a deeply personal way. -*Lejone Morris*